Social Sense
and
Practice

In the same series

Indoor Gardens and Window Boxes Gisela Gramenz
Needle and Thread Ines Ruebel
Restoring Old Junk Michèle Brown

Social
Sense
and
Practice

Hazel Ward

With illustrations by
Belinda Lyon

Lutterworth Press
Guildford and London

First published 1974

To
MY FAMILY

The prayer of welcome quoted on page 130 and the *Ephphetha* quoted on page 131, in the chapter on birth, adoption, and naming ceremonies, are copyright by the International Committee on English in the Liturgy Inc.

ISBN 0 7188 2089 4

Copyright © by Hazel Ward 1974

Text set in 12/13 pt. Photon Imprint,
printed by photolithography,
and bound in Great Britain at The Pitman Press, Bath

Contents

Acknowledgments

I should like to thank Mrs J. Ford, N.F.F., of Buckswood Grange, Uckfield, for her kindness in providing ideal conditions under which to write this book, and, in particular, Mrs T. B. Drew, for her help over many years.

My publishers and I would also like to thank all who helped with the supplying and checking of information for this book, in particular the following:

The British Humanist Association
The British Medical Association
The Ven. Phra Douglas Paññāvaro, of the Buddhist Society
The Church Information Office
The Crown Office, Edinburgh
Fuller & Scott, Funeral Directors of Uckfield, Sussex
General Register Office, Belfast, Northern Ireland
General Register Office, Edinburgh, Scotland
General Register Office, London, England
H.M. Inspector of Anatomy, Department of Health and Social Security
The Home Office
The Incorporated Society of Valuers and Auctioneers
Inner London Executive Council of the National Health Service
The Islamic Cultural Centre
Betty Jones (Travel Editor, *Woman and Home* and *Woman's Weekly*)
The Law Society
Moss Bros. Ltd.
The National Association of Funeral Directors
Mrs Elizabeth Ward of the National Kidney Research Fund
The Office of the Chief Rabbi, London
The Passport Office
The Royal Institute of British Architecture
The Royal Institution of Chartered Surveyors
The Royal National Institute for the Blind
The Scottish Home and Health Department
The Scottish National Federation for the Welfare of the Blind
The Society of Friends
South Place Ethical Society

The information given in this book should not be regarded as being authorised or authenticated by any of these people and institutions; this is merely an acknowledgment of their kindness and helpfulness.

The names used to add a touch of colour in some passages, particularly in the chapter on the Marriage, are all 'made up' for this purpose.

Introductions

Day by day, circumstances arise which necessitate bringing people together. To introduce them is to establish contact on a formal basis. While men and women in their own homes can invite and introduce those of their friends and acquaintances who will, they know, find pleasure and stimulation in each other's company, in other fields it is usually professional, commercial or business matters which dictate their meeting, and a degree of formality is reasonable. In all cases it is important that introductions are effected properly and the names spoken clearly.

Making introductions

The general rule is that except in the case of Royalty (page 12), a man is always introduced to a woman, an unmarried woman to a married one, a younger person to an older. By the same token, an untitled man is presented to one of rank, a bachelor to a married man.

To perform an introduction, simply say, 'Mrs Black, may I introduce Captain Brown?' and then, turning to Captain Brown, 'Mrs Black'; or, 'Lady White, I don't think you have met Miss Green. She is a member of our committee.'

It is always helpful to give the two people introduced an opening for conversation by mentioning some interest they might have in common.

If you are introducing a friend to your parents, he or she should be introduced to your mother first, and then to your father. If you are introducing a relative bearing the same surname as yourself, it is unnecessary to repeat it: 'Mrs Grey, I don't think you have met my brother Frank.' If the name is not the same as your own, however, it should be mentioned: 'Mrs Bell, this is my sister, Mrs Graham.'

A man should not introduce his wife as 'Mrs Jones' nor a wife her husband as 'Mr Brown'. It should be 'My wife Jane', 'My husband John', or 'My husband', 'My wife'.

Acknowledging an introduction

The correct reply to an introduction is 'How do you do.' It is not absolutely essential to shake hands but greater warmth is shown by doing so. In the case of group introductions, a smile and a slight inclination of the head is all that is required. A woman should always be the first to offer her hand in greeting. A handshake should be brief and firm—never lingering, limp, nor yet a demonstration of physical strength.

A man always rises from his seat when introduced to a woman, or should be taken over to where she is sitting. A woman need not rise when introduced to a man unless she feels that by virtue of age or clerical rank he is entitled to special courtesy. This same courtesy should be extended by a younger woman when meeting an older one, and by a girl on being introduced to the parents of her hostess.

Self-introduction

There is an old adage which says 'A lady is never noticed—always discovered', but at crowded parties and business functions it is often difficult to find the hostess, let alone catch her eye, and on such an occasion it would be foolish to await discovery. A guest finding herself in this plight can quite correctly approach any group of people who appear animated and friendly—though not a private conversation or an all-male party—and say with a smile, 'May I join you for a short time as I cannot find my hostess? My name is Jane Brown and I am attached to—', mentioning someone or something which will indicate where she fits into the scene. People approached in this way invariably respond kindly.

Letters of introduction

Letters of introduction are extremely helpful to those moving to a new area or travelling abroad. Such letters should be given with discretion and only when the writer knows the person well enough to offer this assurance without reservation. Otherwise she may be asking friends to sponsor someone who may prove an embarrassment on further acquaintance.

Letters of introduction should normally be brief and concise, bearing only on the presentation. They should be handed or sent to the bearer in an unsealed envelope addressed to the person to whom they are to be presented. The bearer should not present them personally, but should seal the envelope and send it by post or by hand with a covering note to the address on the envelope.

A letter of introduction should be acknowledged without delay, either by a call or an invitation. If this proves impossible, a letter of explanation should be sent to the writer of the letter and to the bearer.

If in the course of a business career, a letter of introduction is instrumental in helping the person concerned to secure a better job or promotion within her firm, the writer should be told at once and thanked most courteously for the help given.

21, Ink Place,
Penfold Avenue,
London, S.W.1.

My dear Barbara,

I am sending this letter by a dear friend of mine, Miss Joy Deeds, who has just moved to a delightful cottage at Burford, within a few miles of Harley Manor. She is a charming person, full of fun and good cheer, and most hospitable. After a very busy life in London as a journalist, she has chosen to desert us all in order to write an historical novel and while this may prove most absorbing, I am sure she would welcome some social contact.

I should be most grateful if you would look in on her soon and perhaps invite her to your own most beautiful home. I remember my own visit to you with great joy and look forward very much to seeing you here in the near future.

Yours affectionately,

Helen

Dear Mrs Little,

I am sending this by a friend of long standing, Mrs Charles Day, who is visiting Palma in search of a summer villa. She hopes to accomplish this in five or six weeks, but knows little of the island, and it would be most kind if you could invite her to your lovely apartment and perhaps put her on the right lines in order to streamline her search.

She is a delightful person and a splendid friend. Her husband is a cousin of Henry Knight whom we both know. They are both warmly hospitable.

I hope you will find time to visit us, however briefly, when you are in England again. In the meanwhile, my love and good wishes to all.

Yours affectionately,

Violet Main

11

Presentation to Royalty

On being presented to Royalty, women curtsey, keeping the back straight and looking upwards; men bow, inclining the head from the neck only. If a conversation is initiated by the royal personage, the first spoken reply is 'Your Majesty' (*or* 'Your Royal Highness'), and thereafter 'Madam' (pronounced 'Mam') or 'Sir'.

Performing a presentation

On formal occasions it is usual for names to be submitted and permission obtained before anyone is presented to Royalty. In making the presentation, the person so doing should say 'Your Majesty (*or* Your Royal Highness), may I present—' giving the name and, if the occasion warrants, a brief reference to the position held, thus, 'Your Majesty, may I present Mrs Mary Hill, the matron of our new crèche?' If a number of people are presented, there is no need to repeat 'May I present' each time, the name and details being sufficient.

Presentation to Royalty does not entail turning to the person presented and repeating the name of the royal person, as does an ordinary introduction.

Royal walkabouts

In the case of a royal walkabout there are no formal presentations, the Queen, Prince Philip and other members of the Royal Family simply walking about among the crowds and stopping for an impromptu conversation or a few words with whoever is nearest to them at that moment. The manner of reply is set out above, but these occasions call for spontaneous unaffected warmth and goodwill rather than careful formality.

Letter-writing

With a car in the garage and a telephone conveniently placed, a good many people feel the urgency for and incentive to letter-writing has gone. Friendships can be kept alive by the spoken word even when meetings are rare; gossip can be exchanged and invitations issued; and should a family crisis arise, a two-hundred-mile car journey can take less time than the delivery of a letter. In business, commerce and industry, the telephone provides such vital links over land and sea that its worth in terms of time and money is inestimable. At a higher level, jet travel can bring government representatives together for negotiation before drafts of protest can be phrased.

Yet, in spite of all these things, the written word is the most powerful and the most potent form of communication used by civilised man. The British Post Office alone handles something in excess of nine thousand million letters and packages every year, and nothing can take the place of this means of setting the seal on the hopes, fears, ideals, orders, opinions and directions of peoples at every level and in every place throughout the world.

To reflect any of these things in writing with sincerity, honesty, efficiency, tact and courtesy, adding that intangible quality which combines style and personality, is the essence of every letter and an accomplishment worth cultivating.

Correspondence generally falls into three categories, social, business and official, and all are necessary in the course of daily life.

Hand-written letters

Social letters fit into two categories—formal and informal—and etiquette requires that all those of a formal nature are hand-written. They include letters offering congratulations (page 16) or condolences (pages 16 and 145); those giving thanks for good wishes, kindnesses and sympathy (page 146); letters of invitation (page 49), letters of introduction to friends (page 11), letters of thanks for visits, dinner parties and formal luncheons (pages 57 and 76).

Informal letters to friends and relatives are usually hand-written, but they can be typed if you know the recipient sufficiently well. In this case, the salutation and the subscription and signature should always be hand-written.

Type-written letters

All business letters are written with a set purpose and this should be stated in clear, concise language without discursiveness. Wherever possible business letters are, and should be, typed so as to avoid illegibility and any misunderstanding. Business letters of introduction should be typed if possible.

Beginnings and endings and signatures

No matter whether letters are social, business or official, it is important that the salutation and the subscription are in harmony with each other. Thus a social letter beginning *Dear Mrs Jones* should end *Yours sincerely,* a warmer note being expressed in letters of friendship beginning *My Dear Anne* and ending *Love from.* Salutations such as *My Love* or *Darling Jane* call for more intimate subscriptions: *Yours affectionately* or *Lovingly Yours.* A social letter beginning *Dear John* and ending *Yours sincerely* can be warmed and softened by writing *With all good wishes* or *With kindest regards* on the line above the subscription.

Business letters beginning *Dear Sir* should end *Yours faithfully.* In the case of tradesmen known personally, the salutation and subscription can be less formal: *Dear Mr Jones . . . Yours truly.*

In writing to strangers, the accepted form is *Dear Sir* or *Dear Madam,* the subscription being *Yours faithfully.*

The practice of writing to business colleagues and acquaintances whom one has met but does not yet know well, or whom one has not yet met but to whom one has already written several times, with the salutation *Dear Anne Smith* and the subscription *Yours sincerely* or merely *Yours* seems at present to be gaining ground as an intermediate stage between *Dear Mrs Smith . . . Yours sincerely* and *Dear Anne . . . Yours.*

The 'Women's Lib' preference for Ms, rather than Miss or Mrs, now becoming established in American business letters, should also be noted.

Official letters addressed to members of the peerage, heads of organisations, civic dignitaries and editors of newspapers, beginning *Sir* should end *I am, Sir, Yours faithfully* although professional letters, as opposed to business letters, should conclude *I am, Sir, Yours truly.*

The section on *The Written and Colloquial Application of Titles and Forms of Address,* on pages 17–31, goes into detail about salutations and subscriptions in business and social letters to Royalty, peers, the professions and so on.

When signing a letter, only the given name and surname, or initials and surname, or the given name alone, is required: *Jane Jones, Joan T. Brown, M. G. White, Malcolm.* It is incorrect to use a title, letters after the name, or the designation *Mr* or *Mrs.* If 'Jane Jones' wishes to clarify her situation as an unmarried woman, she can do so by writing *Miss Jane Jones* in block leters underneath her signature or in the upper corner of the letter over the address, as can Joan T. Brown by writing in the same way *Mrs Charles Brown* and Malcolm White by writing *Mr M. G. White.*

14

Envelopes

Envelopes should be addressed clearly, if necessary in block capitals, with the name, address, town, county and district number. An unmarried woman is designated *Miss Jean Brown* or whatever her name happens to be; a married woman is addressed by her husband's initials *Mrs T. (Tom) Brown*—although she retains her own initials on election lists and on her passport, and sometimes when she is in business. A widow retains her husband's initials and continues to be addressed as *Mrs John Jones*. A divorcée reverts to her given name, while retaining her former husband's surname, thus *Mrs Mary Smith*. Details about addressing envelopes to Royalty, peers, members of the professions and so on, appear in the section on pages 17–31.

Esquires

The courtesy title *Esquire*, dating from medieval times, originally implied a rank slightly above that of gentleman. Although today, were the niceties strictly observed, it should be reserved for serving officers, younger sons of peers, barristers-at-law and a few other classes of 'gentlemen', by common usage it has been adopted as an alternative title to plain Mr. A business communication addressed to a tradesman rightly describes him as *Mr J. Jones,* a social letter designating him *J. Jones Esq.* is equally correct in modern idiom.

'*Master*'

In writing to boys up to the age of six, envelopes can be addressed to 'Master': for example, *Master Peter Piper*. From then on to school-leaving age the given name and surname is sufficient, thus *Jack Johnson*.

Materials and layout

The choice of stationery is important in-so-far as it provides a background for a letter, and plain writing paper in white, grey or azure with dark blue or black ink used in contrast, is in good taste and pleasing to the eye. Deckled-edge paper, lines and pretty colours should be eschewed by adults.

One glance at a newspaper or magazine will serve to show that wide margins, well-defined paragraphs, even spacing and clear lettering all add to the attractive presentation of a letter.

Some sample letters

Letter of congratulations

Dear Bill,

A line to offer my heartiest congratulations on your engagement. I have known Elizabeth for many years and really envy you your good fortune. She is a charming girl with a particularly happy personality. You will find her parents are delightful people, and with such a pleasant home background, Elizabeth cannot fail to carry this over into her own future home.

My good wishes are with you for a wonderful future and a very happy present,

Your old friend——

Letter of sympathy

Dearest Emma,

I was sorry to hear the results of your examination. Knowing how hard you have worked, it must have been a sore disappointment and I am full of sympathy. Try not to be too down-cast as I hear you have another chance in the spring of next year—probably you will sail through then with flying colours. You know that our good wishes will be with you over the coming months, so take heart and look forward to a successful future.

Your ever loving——

Request to see a child's headmistress

Miss G. Brain,
Headmistress,
St George's Primary School,
Barchester.

Dear Miss Brain,

My husband and I are most concerned about our daughter Jenny who seems very unhappy in her school life. Twice last week she returned home in a distressed condition but was unable or unwilling to enlighten us as to the cause of her tears and misery. We are naturally anxious to find out the reason and would be glad to arrange an appointment to call on you as soon as is convenient. We look forward to hearing from you.

Sincerely——

Titles and Modes of Address

Royalty

If one wishes to write to a Member of the Royal Family, unless personally known, it is usual to address the correspondence to the Private Secretary or Lady in Waiting concerned. It is, however, advantageous to know the formal modes of address.

In writing to the Queen, the formal mode of address is to use the superscription *To the Queen's Most Excellent Majesty,* the salutation *Madam* or *Your Majesty,* and the subscription

> *I remain,*
> > *Your Majesty's most faithful servant*

or

> > *I have the honour to remain, Madam,*
> > > *Your Majesty's humble and obedient servant*

The envelope should be addressed:

> > *Her Majesty The Queen,*
> > *Buckingham Palace,*
> > *London, S.W.1.*

If the Court is in residence at Windsor, Balmoral or any other place at the time of writing, letters are forwarded immediately.

The spoken form of address is 'Your Majesty' initially, and thereafter 'Madam' (pronounced 'Mam'). A speech at an official function would begin 'May it please Your Majesty——'

A letter to the Queen Mother would have as its superscription *To Her Majesty Queen Elizabeth The Queen Mother,* the beginning and ending following the lines set out above, and the envelope being addressed to:

> > *Her Majesty Queen Elizabeth The Queen Mother,*
> > *Clarence House,*
> > *St James's,*
> > *London, S.W.1.*

The spoken form of address is the same as that for the Queen.

Only the following are accorded the style of *His (Her) Royal Highness* and are Princes or Princesses of Great Britain:

> Sons and Daughters of the Sovereign
> Sons, Daughters and the eldest surviving Grandson of The Prince of Wales
> Sons of Sons of the Sovereign

The dignity of Royal Highness and Prince or Princess is sometimes accorded by Royal Warrant as in the case of The Queen's Consort.

Wives take the styles and precedence of their husbands: for example, H.R.H. The Duchess of Kent.

The superscription and form of address on envelopes addressed to the members of the British Royal Family vary with the name, title, rank and decorations held. At present they are as follows:

H.M. Queen Elizabeth The Queen Mother
H.R.H. The Prince Philip, Duke of Edinburgh, K.G., K.T., O.M., G.B.E.
H.R.H. The Prince of Wales, K.G.
H.R.H. The Prince Andrew
H.R.H. The Prince Edward
H.R.H. The Princess Anne, Mrs Mark Phillips
Captain Mark Phillips
H.R.H. The Princess Margaret, Countess of Snowdon, C.I., G.C.V.O.
The Earl of Snowdon, G.C.V.O.
H.R.H. The Duke of Gloucester, G.C.V.O.
H.R.H. The Duchess of Gloucester
H.R.H. Alice, Duchess of Gloucester, C.I., G.C.V.O., G.B.E.
H.R.H. The Duke of Kent, G.C.M.G., G.C.V.O., A.D.C.
H.R.H. The Duchess of Kent
H.R.H. Prince Michael of Kent
H.R.H. Princess Alexandra, the Hon. Mrs Angus Ogilvy, G.C.V.O.
The Hon. Angus Ogilvy
H.R.H. Princess Alice, Countess of Athlone, V.A., G.C.V.O., G.B.E.

Except in special and very formal circumstances, however, it is not usual to add decorations to the names of members of the Royal Family, with the exception of K.G. (Knight of the Garter) and K.T. (Knight of the Thistle). Circumstances also dictate whether or not service ranks are used: the Prince of Wales is a serving naval officer, the Duke of Kent and Prince Michael of Kent are serving army officers, and their ranks would accordingly be shown on service documents.

The formal salutation is *Your Royal Highness* or *Sir* or *Madam,* and the subscription

> *I have the honour to be, Sir (Madam),*
> *Your Royal Highness's (humble and) obedient servant*

The spoken address is initially 'Your Royal Highness' and then 'Sir', or 'Your Royal Highness' and then 'Madam' (pronounced 'Mam'). A speech at an official function would begin 'Your Royal Highness———'

In private conversation all Princes bearing the title of *His Royal Highness* are addressed as 'Sir' and all Princesses bearing the title of *Her Royal Highness* as 'Madam' ('Mam'). If, however, one were asking a direct question, 'Your Royal Highness' might be used. A reply to a question from a Prince or Princess should conclude 'Sir' or 'Madam' (pronounced 'Mam'). Only close associates and intimate friends use the terms 'Prince' and 'Princess'. Organisers of functions and committee members addressing Royalty in conversation should use the formal terms.

Peers and Peeresses, Baronets and Knights and Dames, and their families

In Great Britain there are seven degrees of rank which carry a title. They are Duke, Marquess, Earl, Viscount, Baron (or, in Scotland, Lord of Parliament), Baronet and Knight; and their female equivalents. Holders of the first five ranks are noblemen, or 'peers of the realm', and may sit in the House of Lords, which baronets may not do—their only right is that of handing on the title to their heirs. Knighthood and damehood are conferred for life alone, by the Sovereign.

Colloquially, a duke is addressed by his close friends as 'Arun' or 'Middlesex' or whatever his territorial name may be. In social conversation he and his duchess are referred to as 'the Duke' and 'the Duchess', and are addressed as 'Duke' and 'Duchess'. In very formal terms and on very formal occasions, they may be spoken of as 'His Grace' and 'Her Grace', and addressed as 'Your Grace'.

If you are writing to a duke, the salutation depends on the degree of friendship. The very formal salutation and subscription, not widely used nowadays, are *My Lord Duke . . . I remain (my Lord Duke), Your Grace's most obedient servant*. It is more usual to begin formally *My Lord Duke* and conclude *Yours faithfully*; or, socially, *Dear Duke of ——* or *Dear Duke . . . Yours sincerely*. The envelope should be addressed to *His Grace the Duke of ——* (formal) or *The Duke of ——* (social).

Similarly, letters to a duchess begin, according to the degree of formality or friendship, *Madam, Dear Madam, Dear Duchess of ——, Dear Duchess,* and conclude *I have the honour to be, Madam, Your Grace's most obedient servant* (very formal), or, more usually, *Yours faithfully* or *Yours sincerely*. The envelope is addressed *Her Grace the Duchess of ——* (formal) or *The Duchess of ——* (social).

The eldest son or heir apparent of a duke usually takes one of the duke's peerage titles, generally the second, and is addressed accordingly as a peer (see below), although he does not sit in the House of Lords and he (and his wife) will drop the formal prefix *The Most Hon.* (if the courtesy title is that of a marquess), *The Rt Hon.* (if it is that of an earl), or *The* (if it is that of a viscount or a baron), in correspondence. In the peerage of Scotland, however, he is known socially by the courtesy title, but has the legal title *The Master of* ——.

A duke's younger sons hold the courtesy title of *Lord,* used with the given name and the family surname: *Lord John Black,* for example; his wife would be styled *Lady John Black.* The formal mode of address in speech is 'My lord' ('Madam'); in conversation, 'Lord John' ('Lady John'). The very formal manner of address in writing is *My Lord (Madam) . . . I (have the honour to) remain, my Lord (Madam), Your Lordship's (Your Ladyship's) obedient servant;* less formally *My Lord (Dear Madam) . . . Yours faithfully;* socially *Dear Lord John Black (Dear Lady John Black),* or on better acquaintance, *Dear Lord John (Dear Lady John) . . . Yours sincerely.* The envelope is addressed to *Lord John Black (Lady John Black).* Similarly, a duke's daughter holds the courtesy title of *Lady,* used with the given name and family surname: *Lady Helen Black,* for example. The forms of address, in speech and in writing, exactly parallel those just described for the wife of a duke's younger son ('Madam', 'Lady Helen', *Madam, Dear Lady Helen,* and so on). If Lady Helen married a peer, she would take his title (becoming *The Countess of* ——, for example, if she married an earl) but if she married a baronet, a knight, or Mr ——, she would retain the title of *Lady,* used with her own given name, but would change her surname to that of her husband: thus marrying Sir Peter White or Mr Peter White, she would be styled *Lady Helen White.*

It is customary in social terms to address all peers below the rank of duke as 'Lord——' and all peeresses as 'Lady ——'; in formal terms, 'My Lord' and 'Madam'. They are treated as being of equal rank in all matters except precedence (if you are arranging a formal dinner, you will have to check the guest list against the Table of Precedence in the local reference library). Their distinctive titles—*The Marquess of Barchester, The Countess of Silverbridge,* for example—are used only on the envelopes of letters, in newspaper reports, when they are formally announced on entering a room, and on invitation cards and place-name cards.

In writing to a marquess, the very formal salutation and subscription are *My Lord Marquess . . . I (have the honour to) remain (my Lord), Your lordship's obedient servant;* in modern usage, however, *My Lord . . . Yours faithfully;* the envelope being addressed to *The Most Hon. the Marquess of* ——. A social letter begins *Dear Lord* —— and ends *Yours sincerely,* and the words *The Most Hon.* are dropped from the envelope.

The forms of address used in writing to a marchioness parallel those used for a marquess, substituting *Madam* and *Dear Madam* for the very formal and the formal salutations.

The eldest son or heir apparent of a marquess usually takes the marquess's second peerage title, and is addressed accordingly, following the style already described for a duke's heir apparent.

A marquess's younger sons take the title *Lord* with the given name and family surname *(Lord Michael Firth);* their wives are styled accordingly *(Lady Michael Firth).* His daughters similarly take the title *Lady,* used with the given name and family surname *(Lady Anne Firth).* The modes of address in speech and in writing, and the style used by a marquess's daughter after marriage, parallel those given above for the younger sons, wives of younger sons, and daughters of a duke.

In writing to an earl, the formal salutation is *My Lord;* the very formal subscription, the formal subscription, and the social salutation and subscription are as described above for a marquess. A strictly formal letter is addressed to *The Right Hon. the Earl of ——;* on the envelope of a social letter, the prefix *The Right Hon.* is dropped.

The forms of address used to a countess parallel those used for a marchioness.

The eldest son or heir apparent of an earl generally takes the earl's second peerage title and is addressed accordingly, as a viscount or baron, though the formal prefix is not used on a social envelope—he is simply *Viscount Lufton, Baron Mansell,* and so on.

An earl's younger sons are given the courtesy title of Honourable used with the given name and surname—*The Honourable James Wood.* This courtesy title is never used in conversation, or on visiting cards and place-name cards, or even when the holder is formally announced: its only application in writing is on the envelope of a letter. The prefix *Mr* is not used with it. An earl's younger son is thus spoken of as 'Mr Wood', addressed in a formal letter as *Sir* or *Dear Sir* and in a social one as *Dear Mr Wood,* and styled on the envelope *The Hon. James Wood.*

The wife of an earl's younger son is spoken of as 'Mrs Wood', addressed as *Madam, Dear Madam* or *Dear Mrs Wood,* and styled on the envelope *The Hon. Mrs James Wood* (the prefix *Mrs* is used with the courtesy title *Honourable,* though *Mr* and *Miss* are not). If she is of higher social rank than her husband, she uses her own title, without the addition of *Hon.,* but her husband's surname *(Lady Margaret Wood).*

(The courtesy title *Honourable* is also borne by the sons, daughters-in-law, and daughters of viscounts and barons, and precedence depends on the paternal title; anyone arranging a formal function should check accordingly.)

An earl's daughters take the title *Lady,* used with their own given name and the family surname: *Lady Elizabeth Wood.* The forms of address parallel those described for a duke's daughter, as does the changing or retaining of the title on marriage.

In addressing or writing to a viscount, a viscountess, a baron or baroness, on formal or social occasions and in formal or social terms, follow the style already described for an earl and his countess. The formal prefix used on envelopes is *The Right Hon. The Viscount*—— and *The Right Hon. Lord*——; social letters drop the words *The Right Hon.*

The sons, daughters and daughters-in-law of viscounts and barons all have the courtesy title *Honourable,* used with the given name and surname *(The Hon. Christopher Mansell,* his wife *The Hon. Mrs Christopher Mansell,* and his sisters *The Hon. Joanna Mansell, The Hon. Lucy Mansell).* The usual salutations *(Dear Sir, Dear Madam, Dear Mr Mansell, Dear Mrs Mansell, Dear Miss Mansell)* are used, and the usual subscriptions *(Yours faithfully, Yours sincerely).* On marriage the Hon. Joanna and the Hon. Lucy Mansell would keep the courtesy title *(The Hon. Mrs Arne, The Hon. Lady Jones)* unless either married a man of higher rank, in which case she would share his title.

Baronets and knights are addressed in speech by their title and given name—'Sir James'—and referred to by their full name and title—'Sir James Brighton'. A letter begins *Sir, Dear Sir, Dear Sir James Brighton* or *Dear Sir James,* depending on the degree of formality or friendship, and concludes *Yours faithfully* or *Yours sincerely,* as appropriate. If he is a baronet, the envelope is addressed to *Sir James Brighton, Bt*; if he is a knight, the letters indicating which order, and which class within that order, of knighthood has been conferred on him (page 150), should be added after his surname: *Sir James Brighton K.C.B.*

A baronet's wife takes the title of *Lady* with her husband's surname: *Lady Brighton.* She is addressed and referred to socially as 'Lady Brighton', and letters follow the usual *Dear Madam/Dear Lady Brighton, Yours faithfully/Yours sincerely* style, the envelope being addressed to *Lady Brighton.* A baronet's children have no titles.

The forms of address used in speaking, referring or writing to a knight's wife are the same as those for a baronet's. A knight's children have no titles.

The styles of address used for peeresses in their own right parallel those used for the wives of peers, though a baroness in her own right may choose to be addressed as *Dear Baroness* rather than *Dear Lady* ——.

The Order of the Bath, the Order of St Michael and St George, the Royal Victorian Order and the Order of the British Empire may now be conferred on women as well as men. Dames Grand Cross and Dames Commanders of these four Orders are addressed and referred to as 'Dame Jane', 'Dame Mary' and so on. A strictly formal letter opens *Madam* and concludes *I remain, Madam, Your obedient servant;* a formal one, *Dear Madam . . . Yours faithfully;* and a social one, *Dear Dame Jane Lister,* or *Dear Dame Jane . . . Yours sincerely.*

The envelope is addressed to *Dame Jane Lister, G.C.B.* (or *D.B.E.*, or as appropriate).

Dowagers

Generally speaking, a dowager is the earliest surviving widow of the preceding holder of a dukedom, marquessate, earldom, viscountcy or barony. In England, Ireland and Wales, the dowager might well not be directly related to the present holder—she could be his aunt, for example, or his sister-in-law—but in Scotland the title 'Dowager' is reserved for a present holder's mother or grandmother.

A dowager is addressed and referred to in speech and in letters according to the usual styles already outlined, but the word *Dowager* is generally included on the envelope: *Her Grace the Dowager Duchess of Barset* (formal) or *The Dowager Marchioness of Lufton* (social). Some dowagers, however, prefer to use their given name, and if so their wishes should be followed: *Mary, Duchess of Barset.*

While a dowager lives, the widows of succeeding holders of the title similarly use their given name to differentiate them from the wife of the present holder: *Margaret, Marchioness of Lufton.* This style is usually continued for the rest of her life, even if the dowager dies before her.

The government

The Prime Minister and his cabinet ministers are privy councillors and thus bear the title *Right Honourable,* which is accorded to all privy councillors and which is retained for life. (Their wives do not share it.) They are addressed, referred to and written to according to their own rank. Thus if the Prime Minister is a commoner, a formal letter to him opens *Sir (Dear Sir)* and concludes *Yours faithfully,* a social letter opens *Dear Mr Smith* and concludes *Yours sincerely,* and the envelope is addressed to *The Right Hon. Andrew Smith, P.C., M.P., Prime Minister and First Lord of the Treasury.* The salutation and subscription on a letter to a cabinet minister would follow the same lines, the envelope being addressed to *The Right Hon. Peter Port, P.C., M.P.* All members of Parliament are entitled to the letters *M.P.* after their name.

The religious faiths

The Church of England, and the Church of Ireland

An archbishop is addressed on formal social occasions as 'Your Grace' and referred to as 'The Archbishop of ——' or simply 'The Archbishop', not as

'Archbishop Smith'. Formal letters should begin *My Lord Archbishop* and conclude *I have the honour to be, my Lord Archbishop, Your Grace's most devoted and obedient servant;* more social letters may begin *Dear (Lord) Archbishop* and conclude *Yours sincerely.* Envelopes should be addressed *The Most Reverend The Lord Archbishop of* ——. An archbishop's wife has no title in right of her husband's spiritual rank within the Church, and is plain Mrs Smith.

A retired archbishop is addressed and referred to in speech as 'Archbishop Jones'. By courtesy a letter to him still opens *My Lord Archbishop* or *Dear (Lord) Archbishop,* but the envelope is addressed to *The Most Rev. Archbishop Jones.*

If an archbishop or bishop is also a privy councillor, he is styled 'Right Hon.' on the envelope, in addition to his ecclesiastical style.

Bishops are addressed in speech as 'My Lord' or less formally, 'Bishop', and referred to as 'His Lordship'. A formal letter opens *My Lord* and concludes *I have the honour to remain, Your Lordship's obedient servant;* a social one, *My*  *Lord Bishop* or *Dear Bishop . . . Yours sincerely;* the envelope should be addressed to *The Right Rev. The Lord Bishop of* ——. A bishop's wife has no title by right of his spiritual rank. A retired bishop is addressed as 'Bishop Brown'; the envelope is directed to *The Right Rev. Peter Brown.*

A suffragan bishop is addressed in conversation as 'My Lord' and by courtesy this title is also applied in the salutation of a formal letter *(My Lord Bishop)* but the envelope is addressed to *The Right Rev. The Bishop of* ——.

Scottish bishops are addressed by their surnames, not by the name of their diocese: *The Right Rev. Bishop Macdonald.* The Primus is generally addressed as *The Most Rev. The Primus* and called 'Primus'.

Deans are addressed in conversation as 'Mr Dean' or 'Dean'. Letters begin *Very Rev. Sir, Dear Dean, Dear Mr Dean,* depending on the degree of formality, and conclude formally *I have the honour to be, Very Rev. Sir, your obedient servant,* or, in a more social style, *Yours sincerely;* the envelope is addressed to *The Very Rev. The Dean of* ——. A dean's wife has no title, and a dean generally, though not always, reverts on retirement to the ordinary clergy style. If he retains the title, he is addressed as *The Very Rev. John Hill.*

Provosts are addressed in conversation as 'Mr Provost' or 'Provost'. The style of address in writing exactly parallels that of deans.

Archdeacons are addressed colloquially as 'Mr Archdeacon' or 'Archdeacon'. Letters begin *Dear Archdeacon* or *Dear Mr Archdeacon,* concluding *Yours sincerely.* Envelopes are addressed to *The Venerable The Archdeacon of* —— On retirement they customarily drop the title; if they chose to retain it, they are addressed as 'Mr Archdeacon', referred to as 'Archdeacon Vernon', and described on envelopes as *The Venerable Charles Vernon.*

A canon is addressed in speech as 'Canon Peters'. The formal salutation is *Dear Sir* or *Reverend Sir,* but a letter from a friend or acquaintance begins *Dear Canon Peters,* or *Dear Canon.* The envelope is addressed to *The Rev. Canon A. Peters.*

The forms of address used when speaking or writing to a prebendary exactly parallel those used to a canon.

A clergyman is called 'Mr' in conversation, and referred to as 'Mr Green' (although a very formal speech may open 'Reverend Sir' or refer to him initially as 'The Reverend Mr Green'), except where he holds a D.D. (doctorate of divinity) or a D.C.L. (doctorate of clerical learning) in which case he is addressed as 'Dr'. A letter begins *Dear Mr Green* (or *Dear Dr Green* in the latter case). The envelope is addressed *The Rev. Ian R. Green* (or *The Rev. Ian Green, D.D.*).

The Roman Catholic Church
The usual way of addressing the head of the Roman Catholic Church in speech is 'Your Holiness' or 'Most Holy Father'. In writing, a letter begins *Your Holiness* or *Most Holy Father* and ends *I have the honour* (or *the profound veneration) to be, Your Holiness's most obedient servant* (or *child*). The usual way of addressing the envelope is *His Holiness Pope Paulus VI.*

The next ecclesiastical rank below that of Pope is that of Cardinal. The spoken form of address is 'Your Eminence'. Letters begin *My Lord* or *My Lord Cardinal* and conclude *I remain, my Lord, Your Eminence's most devoted and obedient servant* (or *child*); letters from friends and close acquaintances may begin *Dear Cardinal* ——— . . . *Yours sincerely.* The envelope is addressed *To His Eminence Cardinal* ———.

Archbishops are addressed and referred to in speech as 'Your Grace', 'His Grace'. Letters open formally *My Lord Archbishop,* socially *My dear Lord Archbishop,* and conclude formally *I have the honour to remain, my Lord Archbishop, Your Grace's devoted and obedient servant* (or *child*), socially *Yours sincerely.* The envelope is addressed to *His Grace The Archbishop of* ———.

Bishops are addressed and referred to as 'My Lord', 'His Lordship'. Letters open *My Lord, My Lord Bishop, My dear Lord Bishop,* depending on the degree of formality and conclude similarly *I have the honour to remain, Your Lordship's obedient servant* (or *child*), *Yours faithfully, Yours sincerely.* The envelope is addressed to *His Lordship The Bishop of* ———.

Canons, provosts and monsignori are addressed and referred to by their clerical rank and their surname: 'Canon Vaux', 'Monsignore Hardy'. Formal letters open *Very Rev. Sir,* less formal ones *Dear Canon Vaux* or *Dear Monsignore;* they conclude *I have the honour to remain, Very Rev. Sir, Your obedient servant,* or in more social terms, *Yours faithfully, Yours sincerely.*

It has been said that there is no validity in addressing priests of the Roman Catholic Church as 'Father', this title being originally bestowed on monks who had taken the vows of celibacy, poverty and obedience. Nonetheless, the general usage in the Church of Rome is to address and refer to a priest as 'Father——'. Formal letters begin *Dear Rev. Father* and conclude *I beg to remain, your obedient servant* (or *child*); less formally, and more frequently, the salutation *Dear Father——* and the subscription *Yours sincerely* are used. The envelope should be addressed *The Rev. Father——.*

Members of religious orders

Ordained members of religious orders for men, whether Roman Catholic or Anglican, are usually addressed as 'Father' and lay members as 'Brother'; Benedictines are called 'Dom'. The members of some orders retain their surnames, others use the Christian name only, and members should be referred to accordingly—'Father Murphy', 'Father Peter'. Letters may begin formally *Dear Reverend Father,* ending *Yours faithfully;* or more warmly, *Dear Father Andrew . . . Yours sincerely.* The envelope is addressed *The Rev. Andrew Smith* (or *The Rev. Fr Andrew Smith, The Rev. Fr Andrew, The Rev. Dom Andrew Smith*), with the letters signifying the Order to which he belongs (*O.S.B.,* the Order of St Benedict, for example) following his name. The holders of conventual office are usually addressed accordingly: 'Father Abbot', 'Father Superior', 'Father Prior' (*Dear Father Abbot, The Right Rev. The Lord Abbot; Dear Father Prior, The Rev. the Prior;* and so on); Benedictines, however, have a 'Father President' (*Dear Father President; The Right Rev. the Abbot President*).

A sister in Orders is addressed as 'Sister' or 'Sister Mary' and referred to as 'Sister Mary'; a letter usually begins *Dear Sister Mary,* ends *Yours sincerely,* and is addressed to *The Rev. Sister Mary* (or *The Rev. Sister Mary Smith,* if surnames are retained in that Order), with the letters signifying the Order following her name. Benedictine nuns in solemn vows are addressed as 'Dame' or 'Dame Anne' (*Dear Dame Anne, The Rev. Dame Anne Mallory, O.S.B.*). Holders of office are addressed and referred to and written to accordingly: 'Reverend Mother' (*Dear Reverend Mother, The Reverend Mother*), 'Sister Superior' (*Dear Sister Superior, The Sister Superior*); a Benedictine abbess is 'Lady Abbess' (*Dear Lady Abbess, The Right Rev. the Lady Abbess*).

The Church of Scotland

The Church of Scotland is an Established Church, as is the Church of England.
Its leader, the Moderator, is addressed as 'Moderator' or as 'Mr —' ('Dr —' if he
holds a doctorate). A formal letter opens *Right Reverend Sir* and concludes *I remain, Right Rev. Sir, Your obedient servant;* a social one opens *Dear
Moderator, Dear Mr —* and concludes *Yours sincerely.* The envelope is addressed *The Right Rev. The Moderator.* After retirement he is designated *Very
Reverend Sir,* letters open and conclude accordingly, and envelopes are addressed to *The Very Rev. Duncan Monroe.*

The Queen is represented by the Lord High Commissioner to the General
Assembly, who is addressed and referred to as 'Your Grace', 'His Grace'.
Letters open *Your Grace,* conclude formally *Your Grace's obedient servant,*
and are addressed to *His Grace The Lord High Commissioner.*

Clergy are addressed in the same way as those of the Church of England.

The Free Churches

Ministers of the Free Churches are normally addressed as 'Mr —' ('Dr —'),
and letters may open *Dear Sir . . . Yours faithfully,* or *Dear Mr —* (*Dear Dr
—*) *. . . Yours sincerely.* The prefix *Rev.* is often added on envelopes.

The Society of Friends

The Quaker tradition is one of 'plain speech', addressing all men and women
alike, and referring to one another as 'Friend'. It is accordingly usual to address
an envelope to *Timothy Brown,* without adding 'Mr' or 'Esq.'.

British Jewry

The Chief Rabbi is addressed and referred to as 'Chief Rabbi'. A letter opens
Dear Chief Rabbi and concludes *Yours sincerely.* The envelope is addressed
either *The Very Rev. The Chief Rabbi,* or *The Very Rev. Dr. ——.*

Jewish rabbis are addressed and referred to as 'Rabbi ——', or, if they hold a
doctorate, 'Dr —'. Ministers are addressed and referred to as 'Mr —' (or, once
again, 'Dr —') Letters open *Dear Rabbi Cohen,* or *Dear Dr Cohen,* or *Dear Mr
Cohen,* and conclude *Yours sincerely.* The mode of addressing the envelope
parallels that used for clergy of Christian denominations: *Rabbi J. Cohen, The
Rev. Dr J. Cohen,* or, if the rabbi holds a doctorate, *Rabbi Dr. J. Cohen;*
otherwise simply *The Rev. J. Cohen.*

The Muslim Faith

There is no special style of address used for an Imam or any other dignitary of
the Muslim faith. They are normally addressed exactly as other men would be.

The law

The Lord Chancellor, our principal legal dignitary, is styled *The Rt Honourable The Lord Chancellor*. He is usually a peer of the realm, and is addressed and referred to according to his rank. A formal letter to a lord chancellor holding the rank of earl would begin *My Lord* and conclude *I have the honour to remain, my Lord, Your Lordship's obedient servant,* the envelope being addressed either to *The Rt Honourable The Earl of* ——, *Lord Chancellor,* or to *The Rt Honourable The Lord Chancellor*.

The Lord Chief Justice, the Master of the Rolls and the Lord Justices of Appeal are also styled *Right Honourable*. The Lord Chief Justice may be a peer, and if so is addressed accordingly; failing this, he is addressed and referred to as a judge, as are the Master of the Rolls and the Lords Justice of Appeal. Envelopes are addressed to *The Rt Honourable The Lord Chief Justice of England, The Rt Honourable The Master of the Rolls,* and *The Rt Honourable The Lord Justice*—(or according to rank).

The Vice-Chancellor is styled *The Honourable Vice-Chancellor*. Letters should begin *Sir*.

Judges of the High Court—Puisne judges—are addressed as 'My Lord' and referred to as 'Your Lordship' when they are on the judicial bench. In social conversation they are called 'Judge' or 'Sir Peter' (or whatever the given name may be). Formal letters begin *My Lord* or *Sir* and close *I have the honour to be, my Lord* (or *Sir*), *Your obedient servant*. The envelope is addressed either *The Hon. Mr Justice White,* or *The Hon. Sir Peter White*.

A judge of the county court is addressed when on the bench as 'Your Honour' and referred to as 'His Honour'; in social conversation, however, as 'Judge' or 'Judge —'. Letters begin *Dear Judge* or *Dear Judge Robertson*. Envelopes are addressed *His Honour Judge Robertson*. The title *His Honour* is retained after retirement, but an envelope would then be addressed *His Honour Hugh Robertson*.

Justices of the Peace are addressed when on the bench as 'Your Worship'. Formal letters begin *Sir* and conclude *I beg to remain, Sir, Your obedient servant,* the envelope being addressed *The Rt Worshipful John Jones, J.P.* Social letters follow the *Dear Mr Jones . . . Yours sincerely* mode.

In Scotland, judges of the court of session are addressed officially as 'My Lord' and referred to as 'His Lordship'. The usual formal salutation and subscription are used, and the usual social form (*Dear Lord— . . . Yours sincerely*), the envelope being addressed *The Hon. Lord*— Bailies are addressed formally on the bench as 'Your Worship', socially as 'Bailie—' Letters begin *Dear Bailie* — and are addressed to *Bailie J.* —.

Civic dignitaries

There are nineteen Lord Mayors in England: London, York, Liverpool, Manchester, Birmingham, Leeds, Sheffield, Bristol, Newcastle-upon-Tyne, Bradford, Norwich, Hull, Leicester, Nottingham, Portsmouth, Stoke-on-Trent, Plymouth, Oxford, Coventry; three in Ireland—Belfast, Dublin and Cork—and one in Wales—Cardiff. There are also six in Australia: those of Sydney, Melbourne, Adelaide, Perth, Brisbane and Hobart.

The six Australian Lord Mayors, together with the Lord Mayors of London, York, Belfast and Dublin, are styled *Right Honourable* during their terms of office, this being an official and not a personal prefix. Their wives do not share the style. A Lord Mayor is addressed formally as 'My Lord', a Lady Mayoress as 'My Lady'; formal official letters open accordingly, though social ones open according to their own name and rank. The envelope should be addressed *To The Right Hon. The Lord Mayor of* —— A Lord Mayor's wife, or the lady he has chosen to act as his lady mayoress, is addressed as 'Lady Mayoress'; an envelope is directed to *The Lady Mayoress of* —.

The remaining Lord Mayors are addressed and referred to in similar terms, excepting that an envelope is addressed *The Right Worshipful The Lord Mayor of* —.

The mayor of a city is styled *The Right Worshipful The Mayor of* —— He is addressed on the bench as 'Your Worship' and an official letter would begin *Sir* and conclude *I am, Your Worship's most obedient servant.*

Other mayors are addressed as 'Your Worship' when on the bench, and as 'Mr Mayor' in conversation; the salutation and subscription of a formal letter are as for the mayor of a city, but the envelope is addressed *The Worshipful The Mayor of* ——.

The civic heads of Edinburgh, Perth, Dundee, Aberdeen and Glasgow are known as Lord Provosts, and are addressed as 'My Lord' and referred to as 'His Lordship'. Letters usually begin *Dear Lord Provost,* and are addressed to *The Lord Provost of* —, the words *The Right Hon.* being added in the case of the Lord Provosts of Edinburgh and Glasgow. Wives do not share this title. Provosts of other Scottish cities are referred to as 'The Provost', but formal letters begin *Sir*.

Aldermen are addressed on the bench as 'Your Worship' or officially as 'Mr Alderman'. Official letters begin formally *Dear Sir,* and social ones *Dear Mr Alderman* (or *Dear Mr Alderman Brown*). The envelope is addressed *Mr Alderman J. Brown*. An alderman who has a title, however, is styled 'Alderman Sir John Brown'; and so on.

A town councillor should be addressed in writing as *John Blunt, Esq., T.C.*

The universities

University chancellors and vice-chancellors are addressed as 'Sir' or 'Mr Chancellor (Mr Vice-Chancellor)'; official and formal letters begin *Sir* and conclude *I am, Sir, Your obedient servant;* social and less formal ones, *Dear Mr Chancellor (Dear Mr Vice-Chancellor) . . . Yours sincerely;* the envelope being addressed *The Rt Honourable The Chancellor of the University of* —— *(The Rt Worshipful The Vice-Chancellor* etc.). High Stewards and Deputy High Stewards are addressed and written to in an exactly parallel style, the envelope being simply addressed to *The High Steward (The Deputy High Steward) of the University of* ——.

The title by which the head of a college is known varies, and one must check in advance whether it is Master, Mistress, President, Principal, Provost, Rector, Warden. The usual formal address may be used in speech or in writing; social letters may begin *Dear Master of* ——, or more simply *Dear Master;* the envelope being addressed *The Master of* —— *College,* or *The Master,* —— *College.*

Professors are addressed in conversation as 'Professor —', and in social letters as *Dear Professor* —, the envelope reading *Professor M. C. Peters.* Holders of doctorates are addressed as 'Dr —', letters begin *Dear Dr* —, and the envelope reads *Giles Shaw, Esq., Ph.D., Dr. Giles Shaw,* or *Mrs Mary Shaw, D. Litt.*

The medical profession

Doctors are addressed as 'Doctor Mayne', and letters open *Dear Dr Mayne.* The direction on the envelope includes the principal relevant medical degree or qualification, thus *James Mayne, Esq., M.D.* (or *James Mayne, Esq., F.R.C.S.*). Surgeons, however, are addressed as 'Mr'.

Decorations, Honorifics, etc.

In the list of abbreviations that may follow a man's or woman's name, those indicating honours and decorations come first, then degrees, then other distinctions such as R.A. (Royal Academician) or F.R.S. (Fellow of the Royal Society).

Membership of one of the higher ranks in an Order, such as the Royal Victorian Order, automatically includes membership of the lower ranks, but only the highest held should be indicated. A woman who has held the distinction of being an Officer of the Order of the British Empire (O.B.E.) and who is then awarded that of being a Commander (C.B.E.) is accordingly addressed as *Miss Smith, C.B.E.,* not *Miss Smith, C.B.E., O.B.E.*

Professional qualifications such as degrees (D. Litt., for example) and abbreviations indicating official status (J.P., for example) should be used if one is writing in a professional or official capacity. Military decorations should always be included when writing to serving members of the armed forces. The abbreviations *M.P.* (member of Parliament) and *Q.C.* (Queen's Counsel) are used in general as well as professional correspondence.

The accepted order of precedence for the use of honours, decorations, and so on, is given on page 150.

Inviting and Introducing a Speaker

The invitation

An invitation to a speaker should include a choice of dates and a clear indication as to how long she is expected to speak. She should also be asked the amount of her fee or told what the organisers are prepared to offer. Make it clear whether this includes expenses. The secretary should obtain notes on the speaker's work and achievements for the benefit of the chairman, and further details which by consent may be issued to the Press, and should find out what equipment, if any, the speaker requires. A sample letter of invitation appears below.

If the speaker is travelling by train, arrangements should be made to meet her at the station; if by car, a watch should be kept for her arrival; parking and cloakroom facilities should be laid on. Where a speaker is good enough to waive a fee, flowers or some other token gift should be offered as a small gesture of appreciation. At an ordinary assembly, the speaker is usually the guest of honour and her place on the platform should be on the right of the chairman.

Dear Lady Hands,

As a Committee Member of the Charlsworth Archaeological Society with responsibility for programme planning, I am writing to ask whether it would be possible for you to be our Guest Speaker on April 24th or May 22nd of this year.

The Society was formed three years ago and we now have a flourishing membership of six hundred. I enclose press cuttings which will give you a clear picture of our achievements locally, our associations further afield and our hopes for the future, which include the possibility of a trip to Northern Greece and a brief participation in the Athenina Project. Your own writings on this are well-known and we should be delighted to hear you speak on it, or on any other allied subject which you feel would be of interest to our members. Meetings are at 8 p.m. in the Garden Rooms at the Town Hall; a microphone and a slide projector are available there, and we would be happy to obtain any other equipment you needed; speaking time is usually 45 minutes: our fee in this case a suggested £15.75, plus expenses, which we hope will be acceptable.

We shall look forward to hearing from you and if you can fit us into your very busy schedule, perhaps you would let us have such details of your work and travels as can be used briefly by our Chairman in his introductory remarks, and for press releases.

With all good wishes,
Yours sincerely,

Mrs Edward Brown

The introduction

A chairman introducing a speaker should be brief and to the point, and he should welcome her warmly, state her name clearly, and give such details of her past and present work and achievement as will indicate to the audience why she is standing there. Beyond that a Chairman is trespassing as when a busy, popular person has given of her time and energy to speak in support of any cause, she expects, and is entitled to, the floor. Five minutes is time enough for any introductory remarks.

The vote of thanks

A vote of thanks is that gesture of courtesy always extended to a speaker at the end of her talk. The proposer and the seconder should be advised in advance that this slight social 'up-lift' will be theirs. No lengthy speech is required, but the proposer should be in a position to pick out a few salient points made by the speaker, for whereas the chairman's duty is to promote interest in the speaker herself, the one selected to propose the vote of thanks should focus interest on what she has said. Three minutes is long enough: the proposer begins traditionally with the words 'Mr Chairman (Madam Chairman), Ladies and Gentlemen' and could well continue 'I am delighted to have this opportunity of expressing our appreciation of the thought-provoking (amusing, delightful, excellent, instructive) talk given by Mrs Green' (here the proposer should single out one or two main points and dwell on them for a minute or so) and conclude by saying, 'I have much pleasure in proposing a vote of thanks to our speaker, Mrs Green.'

The seconder should adopt the same technique, but beyond a few appreciative words, should confine himself or herself to saying, 'It is with great pleasure that I second the vote of thanks to Mrs Green.' The speaker may like to make a brief reply and the Chairman should then bring the proceedings to an end.

Business Etiquette

The executive

The world of business and commerce is a hard, competitive sphere for the woman who sets her sights at executive level and she needs not only a sound training and knowledge of her job, but tough resilience, a cool head and a clear mind. She also needs charm of manner, assurance, dignity, a good appearance and the dexterity to keep her business life and her private life in separate compartments, merit being independent of sex. Odd pockets of sex discrimination still linger, and the board room often stacks a weight of prejudice behind its closed doors, but gradually enlightened companies are conceding a place here and there on the correct assumption that the high-calibre woman executive is gilt-edged stock in her own right and worth acquiring.

Clothes are important to any woman: to the woman executive they are a part of her public image. She can afford the best and should at all times dress correctly for the meeting or function she attends, choosing those simple well-cut clothes which can be worn with effortless grace and dismissed from her mind directly they are put on.

The woman executive should be discreet in speech and manner, avoiding all situations which reflect adversely on her business or private life: she should not involve herself in transitory affairs of the heart with those she meets within her professional orbit, nor damage her reputation by promiscuity. She should eschew discussion on company affairs outside its offices, and be reticent about her private life inside of them.

The secretary

The secretary, whether the product of a first-class business college, merit promotion or university, has an exciting and exacting role to fulfil and the first requirements of her job are competence and discretion. The secretary/employer relationship can be difficult or it can be pleasant, but it can never be entirely relaxed. It can be friendly, but never familiar: there should be respect on both sides but never apprehension on hers. Since both are human they will make mistakes; the secretary must not be afraid to admit hers, and with tact and diplomacy, point out his. The good secretary must act as a buffer between her boss and the outside world, but never as a barrier. She should have the confidence of the inner sanctums and of the general office and betray neither. Confidential papers and correspondence which the secretary is privileged to handle should be regarded as a sacred trust, as should confidential meetings and interviews. Her telephone manner should be impeccably courteous and helpful.

The secretary's dress should be as discreet as her manner. Speculation inside a city office should be geared to stocks and shares, not the female cleavage. Needless to say, a secretary should never enter into any relationship with her boss which might cause gossip or scandal.

The general office

Many women do not aspire to executive or secretarial status and are content to use their skills and capabilities to good effect at a more modest level, often combining a business or professional life with that of home-maker, and making a marked success of both careers. Women so engaged are not competing for high stakes and are content to remain anonymous and unsung so long as the valuable contribution they make is recognised realistically from a financial angle. They are polite, helpful and pleasant to each other and to any strangers they meet in the course of their duties. They are also dependable and flexible, not being afraid to take on the work of others in an emergency. In many cases they are responsible for the initial training of junior staff and do this competently and without rancour even when it slows down their own work output. Their quiet efficiency and code of etiquette is worthy of note and commendation.

Juniors

Every girl setting out to make a living has to start somewhere and unless qualifications are exceptional, that place is at rock-bottom. It *isn't* easy for any girl leaving school to realise that she is junior material once more, subject to receiving orders and perhaps being pushed around. It *is* easy to get the idea that jobs are two a penny and can be picked up anywhere without effort—so they can if a girl's imagination takes her no further than a weekly wage packet which will cover tights and the latest pop hit. For those who think further ahead and are determined to get on, the way is open right to the top, though hard work, discipline and determination are the necessary adjuncts to success. Punctuality is important: when one has accepted a job on the premise that there are so many working hours in the day, it is dishonest to shirk them, just as it is dishonest to spend hours in the cloakroom fixing make-up, or on the office telephone making personal calls.

Good manners are necessary in any community which hopes to live at peace within itself and restraint and tolerance are valuable exercises in self-discipline. A junior should never address her superiors by their Christian names until and unless asked to do so. (Even those in senior positions who have close business relationships with managerial staff customarily use a formal approach at office level.) It is unwise to make disparaging remarks about other staff or the firm as a whole, even though she may secretly think of her immediate superior as an 'old hag', and the management as 'fuddy duddy'. A pleasant and helpful manner, a warm smile, a well-modulated telephone voice, tact and diplomacy together with punctillious application, are the assets which will set even the most junior member of staff on the road to success, and it is worth-while staying the course long enough for these qualities to be recognised.

Sample letters

Application for job

The Advertiser,
Box No. 1234,
The Daily Telegraph,
Fleet Street,
London, E.C.4.

(Date)

Dear Sirs,

In reply to your advertisement in today's Daily Telegraph, I wish to apply for the position of Junior Secretary.

I am seventeen years of age and was educated at St. Brandon's High School, Knightsbridge, gaining G.C.E. 'O' level in six subjects with credits in English Language and Commercial subjects. I have just completed a secretarial course at St Leofric's College, Kensington. My speeds are: shorthand 100 words per minute; typing 60 words per minute. I have been taught audio and duplicating and can take dictation straight on to the typewriter with accuracy. I speak German and French and can apply these in commercial terms. I enclose a copy of a testimonial from my Headmistress and one from the Principal of St Leofric's, and should be glad to send you the names of two other people who have known me for some years and would testify to my character.

I should be happy to come for an interview at any time convenient to you and hope my application is of interest to you.

Yours faithfully,

Hand-written applications are often required from school-leavers. Advertisers may also request a *curriculum vitae (c.v.)*, which is a brief account in tabular form setting out the applicant's name, address, nationality, date of birth, with details of her education, training, qualifications and any earlier jobs she has held, giving addresses, dates and grades as necessary, and the names, addresses and professions of her referees (usually two). This should, if at all possible, be typed, unless the advertisement specifically asks that it be hand-written, and should be sent with a brief covering note.

36

Will you be my referee

The Rev. A. B. West,
The Vicarage,
Eastwood Church,
Southwood.

(Date)

Dear Mr West,

As I have now left St Leofric's Secretarial College, I am hoping to secure a first position as Junior Secretary with a firm in London and have applied for such a post today. As this was advertised under a Box No. I cannot yet give you the name, but it is very probable that they and others will ask me to supply the names of one or two people to whom I am well-known and to whom reference can be made.

I should be very grateful if you would grant me permission to give your name for this purpose as I feel that having known me for most of my life, you are able to speak with authority. I assure you, you will have no cause to regret any help you can give.

Yours sincerely,

Giving a reference

Anyone asked to act as a referee should feel free to refuse; indeed it is normally better to do so than to make any derogatory remarks in a reference. Thank the person concerned for asking you, but make some courteous excuse: 'I have made it a rule not to act as a referee; rightly or wrongly, I don't feel this is a role I can take on, even for someone for whom I have a high regard'; or, if the person making the request knows that you have acted as a referee in the past, 'I am so sorry, but I seem to have over-extended myself lately, so I decided recently that I must cut down on my correspondence; I have had to refuse a number of requests, and feel I mustn't make any exceptions.'

If, however, you are willing to act, you should reply immediately to the firm's request for a reference. Write briefly and simply, saying how long you have known the person concerned, and in what capacity, why you think they are suited for the post, and what particular qualities they have. Mark the envelope *CONFIDENTIAL;* head the reference too *CONFIDENTIAL* and date and sign it.

The interview

Young people attending for interviews should, like their seniors, arrive punctually. As far as their wardrobes permit, they should dress with an eye to convention rather than effect, and they should be clean and well-groomed. A good many people tend to perspire when nervous or under stress and the use of a deodorant after bathing is recommended. It is better to smell wholesome rather than exotically female at an interview. When called into the office, smile, shake hands, stand up until asked to sit down, and do not smoke unless a cigarette is offered. Let the interviewer do the talking and look interested in what is being said. Often nervousness is mistaken for boredom and concentration on future possibilities can stimulate to the point of animation. Having said his piece, the interviewer will then ask relevant questions and provide the opportunity for the applicant to ask for any further information she requires about the job, conditions of employment and future prospects. It is unlikely that any immediate decision will be made and usually the interview is brought to an end with the assurance that the applicant will be informed within a certain time whether or not she has secured the position applied for. She should then rise, shake hands once more and leave the room without delay.

Changing jobs
Any woman for whatever reason may feel at one point or another in her career that the time has come to make a change. It may be that she has outgrown her job or her financial commitments have outstripped her salary growth, or the prospects of promotion are so remote that ennui has stifled ambition.

There is always an open market for the well-experienced business woman under forty—after that she may find things a little more difficult—and life is too short anyway to risk premature death by boredom. Nevertheless some thought must be given to a line of action best calculated to improve matters without sacrificing future benefits for immediate gain, and it is often worth-while, before beginning the round of agencies and answering advertisements, to talk things over with the present employers. Staff wastage is a serious matter and management and personnel officers are concerned that employees should find conditions sufficiently attractive to remain, or to talk over their dissatisfaction.

The correct approach is to make an appointment with the management or personnel officer through an immediate superior. If money is the root cause of trouble, facts and figures to support a request for an increase should be marshalled and put forward politely and realistically. Other reasons should be set out in the same way. If the results of the interview prove negative, an employee is within her rights to express the hope that the firm will support any application for employment which is addressed elsewhere.

Dismissal
The right of hire and fire is a power best vested in those who by virtue of age, experience and humanity can wield it with finesse, skill and compassion. To administer the sack to anyone is an unpleasant undertaking—to be on the receiving end is a painful experience at best and those administering the blow should

never forget that human dignity is involved; that a person's present is shattered and their future rendered uncertain.

Older folk should be treated gently and given some form of monetary compensation such as will help over a transition period. Others who have failed to make the grade, or whose faces simply don't fit, should be told honestly where they have gone wrong. Everyone has the right to know why they are being dismissed but the manner of telling should be such as will not destroy but allow them to proceed with added wisdom and as good a reference as is possible under their given circumstance. To dissemble is to demean both parties. Those who receive their discharge should never whine but accept the situation with dignity. A change of direction, however unwanted at the time, often leads to a wider landscape and better opportunities.

Most people are now protected against unfair dismissal and employees usually receive a Contract setting down terms of service at the time of their engagement.

Telephone Manners

Business calls

It is a strange paradox that while large industrial, commercial and business empires spend vast sums of money on promoting a good public image and bedecking their reception areas with luxury furnishings, they turn a blind eye and ear to the often abysmal quality of their most important, though unseen, first line of communication with the outside world—the telephonist. The telephone can be a frustrating instrument at the best of times and if it is manned by abrupt, badly-spoken young women whose sole aim seems to be as rude as possible, as unhelpful as possible and as raucous as possible, then indeed an intolerable climate is generated which must result in loss of money and goodwill all round. Yet a telephonist with a pleasant speaking voice of low timbre is a most valuable asset to any firm and if her manner matches her voice, her price is above rubies and she should be paid accordingly.

The telephone should be answered promptly and the number and the name given: '123 456 Jones and Black here. Can I help you?' If the person or department is not available, the telephonist should say so: 'I'm afraid the number you require is engaged at the moment. Will you hold or can I call you back?' If the caller elects to hold, she should be reassured from time to time that her call is still on hand, so that she does not feel neglected or abandoned. If she has given her name, it should be used, 'I'm so sorry to have kept you waiting, Mrs Brown, I'm putting you through to Mr Jones now.'

All subscribers should remember that exasperation, anger, boredom and insolence lie in a tone of voice which is magnified dramatically over the telephone.

Home calls

In answering the telephone at home, state the number and the name: '567 891 Jill Brown speaking' (a man would use his surname only: '567 891 Brown speaking'). This eliminates cross-talk about wrong numbers and saves time and money. If a wrong number is dialled, the caller should apologise, 'I'm so sorry, I'm afraid I've got the wrong number.'

However intriguing a cross-line conversation may sound, it is ill-mannered to listen in on it, so hang up at once and try again later.

If you are interrupted by a call and want to cut short a conversation before it gets into full spate, say tactfully that the family is about to sit down to a meal or that guests have just arrived.

40

The Professions

In approaching the professions it is necessary to observe certain formalities and conventions, as these skilled and qualified men and women are bound by the inflexible rules of conduct embodied in their statutes.

The medical profession

It is in every woman's interest to see that she and her family are on the registration list of a doctor within her area of residence, whether as a private patient or on the National Health. A list of doctors providing treatment under the National Health Service can be found at the office of the Family Practitioner Committee for the area, and at the Post Office, Public Library, Town Hall, and so on. If you change your address you may choose a new doctor from those listed in the new area by completing part A on page 3 of your medical card and handing it for signature to the doctor who agrees to accept you. Should you wish to continue to receive treatment from your present doctor you should notify him of your new address immediately and establish that he is willing to retain you as a patient.

If you need treatment in an accident or emergency, you should try to get treatment from your own doctor first. If, however, he is not available or if you are at the time not on the list of any doctor, immediate treatment can be obtained from any doctor giving general medical services under the National Health Service.

Should a National Health Service patient wish to change her doctor for any reason other than change of residence, she can either call on the present doctor and ask him to complete the appropriate clause on her medical card, or can send the medical card to the address on the front page, with a note expressing the desire to change. In this case it is not necessary to name the new doctor. The medical card will be returned in due course with instructions on how to proceed.

A private patient unhappy with her treatment and wishing to change her doctor should write a polite note on the following lines:

Dear Doctor Jones,

After much thought, and with regret, I have decided to seek medical advice elsewhere. I do not appear to be making progress and I hope that a change of treatment may restore my confidence and my health.

I shall, of course, pay your account directly it is received.

With thanks for your past care and interest,

Yours sincerely ———

Thus the patient is free to approach another practitioner. The same procedure can be adopted by a National Health Service patient, though in this case there will be no reference to an account.

Should medical treatment be required whilst on holiday or whilst away from home for a period of less than 3 months application can be made for acceptance as a temporary resident to any doctor providing general medical services under the National Health Service in that locality.

The opinion of a specialist or consultant is usually sought by agreement with, and through, a patient's own doctor who will make the appointment and send an accompanying letter containing details of the case. A doctor cannot refuse to let a private patient see a consultant of her choice, although he may discourage the step. Specialist fees are payable in cash or by cheque at the time of the consultation except where the visit is arranged under the auspices of the National Health Service when no fees are payable by the patient. Under the National Health Service, it is for a doctor to decide whether to refer a patient to the hospital and specialist services, and he should do so when he regards this as medically appropriate and necessary.

The General Medical Council (address given on page 153) deals with legitimate complaints of unprofessional practice made against doctors by private patients. Those registered with National Health Service doctors should address their complaints to their local Family Practitioner Committee, whose address is on the Medical Card.

All practising doctors are registered with the General Medical Council.

The legal profession
Solicitors are best approached through the recommendation of friends and this should be followed by a personal letter to the firm or one of the partners asking for an appointment. Having heard the facts of the case or problem, the firm will decide whether they can act for the client. Should litigation be in progress and a new area of residence or dissatisfaction necessitate a change of solicitor, a polite letter should be sent to the acting one, informing him that his services are no longer required. It is unethical for a solicitor to take over a case which is still officially in the hands of another. When this position is clarified, and subject to the payment of any outstanding fees, all documents pertaining to the client's case will be forwarded to the new man.

A good solicitor can be retained for the whole of a lifetime, although it is not always politic for several members of a family to retain the same solicitor.

Where a woman finds herself at odds with the law and has neither a solicitor not money to employ one, she should consult the list—to be found at the local Town Hall or Citizens' Advice Bureau—of solicitors acting on a Legal Aid basis. Appointments to see them can be made for certain days of the week.

Complaints against solicitors should be made in writing to The Law Society, (address on page 153) but *only* when there is evidence of serious malpractice and gross unprofessional conduct.

Barristers are always approached through a solicitor.

Wills

People are apt to put off making a Will thinking there is plenty of time, or that they won't leave enough to worry about anyway; nonetheless, it is always wise to make a Will, and preferable to do so while you are young and in good health.  If you die without leaving a Will, your next-of-kin will be faced with the legal complications of applying for letters of administration, as described on page 147, and your property will be distributed according to the strict rules laid down by Act of Parliament—and the law on this point is inflexible.

Will forms are available from most stationery shops, and if you wish you can buy one and write out your Will and get it signed and witnessed; but it is very much better to get a solicitor to draw it up for you. A solicitor can take into account many possibilities which never occur to the layman, set out exactly what you want done, and fulfil all the necessary legal conditions. The rules about drawing up a Will are strict and it is easy for a layman to make a mistake. There will, of course, be a fee; but as lawyers point out they make far more money sorting out home-made Wills than ever they do out of drawing up proper ones.

You will be asked to name your executors. It is usual to choose two, and to ask them first if they would be willing to be nominated; and it is generally best to choose someone capable who is either your contemporary or rather younger than yourself. Executors are often members of the family or close friends, and it is perfectly in order for them to receive bequests under the Will, though the two people chosen to witness your signature to the Will are not allowed to benefit in any way. Your solicitor will often be willing to act as one of the executors.

If you make your Will before you marry, you must make a new Will on marriage, unless the Will specifically states that it was drawn up with the forthcoming marriage in prospect and taking it into full account.

A note about the process of donating one's eyes, one's kidneys or one's body for transplants or research after death is given on page 149. Arrangements should be made well in advance, and one's executors informed.

Executors are not required to retain the solicitor who drew up the Will.

The clergy

By virtue of their calling, members of the clergy must be permitted to extend the boundaries of etiquette to encompass those situations which do not arise or are not within the experience of other professional bodies.

In asking the clergy to perform any service, it is courteous to request, not demand. It must be noted, too, that many clergymen are reluctant to christen the children of non-practising Christians and it can no longer be assumed they will do so. Parents should ask for an interview with the parish priest or minister to discuss this before going ahead with other arrangements connected with the christening. It must also be realised that a parishioner cannot invite an outside clergyman to officiate at a wedding, a baptism or funeral in the church of another incumbent without that incumbent's agreement, and his permission must be sought. Such permission is seldom refused, but the arrangement is subject to the fee being paid to the incumbent of the parish, not to the visitor.

Architects

Personal recommendation through friends is the most satisfactory way of finding an architect, or the perusal of those monthly or weekly magazines which feature articles on new and interesting houses and developments. Architects' names are usually appended and addresses can be obtained by writing to the magazine in question.

Alternatively the Clients' Advisory Service of the Royal Institute of British Architects (page 153) provides a free information service, designed to assist clients on the selection of architects for specific jobs. The Advisory Service staff will be pleased to discuss your project with you and to suggest three or four firms of architects which you might approach. When you have the names of some architects, try to look at a building they have designed and, if possible, talk to their clients. Above all choose an architect with whom you feel you can build up a good working relationship.

In neither case will the R.I.B.A. recommend a particular architect, as this would be deemed unethical.

It is worth noting that in engaging the services of an architect, there is no binding agreement which compels a client to retain him should he prove unsatisfactory, although of course such work as he has done must be paid for. An insight into costs can be gained from a booklet called *Conditions of Engagement and Scale of Professional Charges,* which is obtainable from R.I.B.A. Publications Ltd (page 153). There is a definite minimum scale of charges which prevents one architect's undercutting another, but no maximum scale is laid down.

Estate agents

Today the choice of an estate agent is governed to some extent by the property advertised in local and national newspapers and that which is displayed with photographs and detailed information in the windows of estate agents offices throughout the country. Recommendation is useful, but on the whole buyers tend to shop around before committing themselves, and indeed they can be on the mailing lists of a dozen agents if they so wish at no cost to themselves. The vendor, too, can shop around and in the South it is normal practice for him to put his property in the hands of more than one agent though in the Midlands and the North sole agency is the commonly recognised practice. He may prefer to approach an estate agent only when he has failed to find a buyer himself by private effort and advertising—and who could blame him for that, since he must pay a commission on whatever price the agent obtains for his property. The function of the estate agent is to act as intermediary between vendors and buyers, but since the vendor is paying the commission, it is up to the negotiator to obtain the best possible price for him. Therefore even when the transaction has reached an advanced stage, should a better offer come along the estate agent must consult his client as to whether to pursue the first or the second course. This often results in disappointment and disillusionment for the would-be buyer. But, although the vendor represents the financial reward of the estate agent, without a steady flow of buyers he cannot function. Irate vendors who chafe because an estate agent does not accomplish in a few days what they have failed to do privately in as many weeks or months, should bear in mind that while an agent can do everything possible to attract applicants he cannot bring them by force into his office, nor make the ultimate decision for them.

Both buyers and sellers for their own safety, should ensure that they are dealing with estate agents who are members of a recognised body such as the Royal Institution of Chartered Surveyors or the Incorporated Society of Valuers and Auctioneers, both of which share in a Joint Indemnity Scheme for safeguarding deposits held by their members on behalf of vendors or purchasers, and each should employ his own solicitor to deal with the legal side of the transaction such as conveyancing and matters arising thereof; indeed the Law Society has recently ruled that a solicitor may not now act for both parties—unless there has been a professional association with each prior to the present transaction.

V.A.T.

With the abolition of a recognised scale of fees, many estate agents have introduced a new system of charges, whereby the percentage varies from a flat rate on the whole of the selling price, to a staggered fee on the amount obtained. Buyers, sellers and those seeking estimates on property are strongly advised to ascertain in advance whether V.A.T. is included in the charges—in many cases it is not and may prove an unpleasant addition to the original quotation. Vendors should also find out whether advertising costs are inclusive, and whether there are other 'hidden' charges and how these are applied.

45

Sending, Accepting and Refusing Invitations

Invitations of an informal nature are now issued by telephone and can be accepted or declined in the same manner. All written, engraved, or printed invitations should receive a hand-written reply.

Invitations for weddings and formal dinner parties are issued in the names of the host and hostess—all others are sent out in the name of the hostess only. In all cases the envelopes are addressed to the lady of the house and not to husband and wife.

Wedding invitations are usually engraved in copperplate writing or printed on a double folded sheet of thick white paper. The guest's name should be hand-written in the top left-hand corner. These should be sent out from three to six weeks in advance of the wedding. Although it is not obligatory to send an invitation to the bridegroom's family, or to the best man and the bridesmaids, as it is taken for granted that they will attend, it is usual for the bride's mother to do so with a covering note saying she is sure they would like to receive one as a memento of the occasion.

Captain and Mrs. Richard Bransome
request the pleasure of
your company at the marriage
of their daughter
Vivienne
to
Mr. John Burns
at St. Paul's Knightsbridge
on Thursday, April 12th
at 4 o'clock
and afterwards at
The Westbury Hotel

R.S.V.P.
8 The Close
Barchester
Barsetshire

Replies should be sent to the bride's mother as speedily as possible so that she can let the caterers know the number of guests who will be at the reception. An acceptance should be couched as follows:

Mr and Mrs Edward Smith have much pleasure in accepting the kind invitation of Captain and Mrs Bransome to the marriage of their daughter Vivienne at St Paul's Church, Knightsbridge, on April 12th, and afterwards at The Westbury Hotel.

A refusal should read:

Mr and Mrs Edward Smith thank Captain and Mrs Bransome for their kind invitation to the marriage of their daughter on April 12th and regret that owing to a previous engagement, they are unable to attend.

Where the parents are divorced and the bride's mother has re-married the invitations should be printed to meet the circumstances, thus:

Mr John Jones and Mrs Thomas Brown
request the pleasure of your company
at the marriage of
their daughter
Jane Anne
etc.

The same rules apply where the bride's father has re-married, but in this case, the mother's style should be Mrs Mary Jones, so that she is distinguished from the second Mrs John Jones.

The parents of a young widow are usually happy to issue the invitations for their daughter's re-marriage. An older widow may prefer to send out her own invitations. Any good stationer will advise on the style and lay-out. They should read as follows:

Mrs Allan Black requests the pleasure of your company at St David's Church, Emsley Road, S.W. 7., at 12 noon on Thursday, March 14th on the occasion of her marriage to Mr James White.

A divorcée can also issue her own invitations, styling herself Mrs Mary Jones as opposed to Mrs John Jones.

Widows and divorcées who are limiting guests to the immediate family and close friends, may like to send hand-written notes of invitation instead of printed cards.

If the bride and groom prefer a very quiet wedding, attended by close friends and relatives only, the invitation is usually phrased as shown overleaf:

Mr and Mrs James Smith
request the pleasure of your company
at the wedding reception of their daughter
Sara Jane
and
Mr John Clark
at The Royal Hotel, Barchester,
on Saturday 19 October
at
three o'clock

R.S.V.P.
2, The Close,
Barchester

Formal dinner party invitations should be engraved in copper-plate writing on a plain white card, or can be hand-written in the third person:

Mr and Mrs Edward Grey
request the pleasure of
the company of
Mr and Mrs David R. Ward
at dinner on
Tuesday 12th June
at 8 o'clock

R.S.V.P.
Hillsborough Lodge,
Court Close,
Richmond.

Black Tie

Replies to formal invitations should be hand-written in the third person:

Mr and Mrs David R. Ward thank Mr and Mrs Edward Grey for their kind invitation to dinner on Tuesday, June 12th at 8 p.m. and have much pleasure in accepting.

A formal refusal should be written in the same manner:

Mr and Mrs David R. Ward thank Mr and Mrs Edward Grey for their kind invitation to dinner on Tuesday, June 12th, but regret that owing to a previous engagement, they are unable to accept.

In these days of informal entertaining, however, most people buy plain 'At Home' cards, filling in their names and writing that of their guest in the top left-hand corner, with the day and date on the line immediately below the *At Home*. If the hostess is an habitual party giver, she may like to have these printed with her name at the top and her address in the bottom left-hand corner, with spaces left for the time, the date and the name of the guest.

An evening *At Home* can take many forms: a sherry, cocktail, or cheese and wine party. In completing the cards, the type of party should be written in the bottom right-hand corner—*Cocktails*—and in the bottom left-hand corner, above the address, *R.S.V.P.,* so that the guests are reminded how essential it is that the hostess knows the number of guests she must cater for. Replies should reach her within forty-eight hours.

Invitations to informal parties, when not telephoned or issued by card, can be hand-written:

Dear Mrs Brown,
   We are inviting a few friends to dine with us on Wednesday April 24th at 8 p.m. and shall be delighted if you and Mr Brown can join us.

The reply, again hand-written, should be on these lines:

Dear Mrs Jones,
   Very many thanks for your kind invitation for the 24th. My husband and I will be delighted to dine with you on that evening at 8 p.m.

Where invitations are issued well in advance of the party, some hostesses send out reminder cards.

Table Manners

Eating can be a crude business without the formality of basic table manners and it is particularly important that some rules are observed if the act of consuming food is to be made more attractive. Children learn by force of example, and quite apart from food, the family board is the first venue of social training.

All members of the family should appear at the table looking clean and tidy. Hands should be washed before and after meals. Table napkins should be opened gently—not with a flourish—and spread across the lap. After family meals, they should be folded and placed in the rings provided. A guest staying in a private house or at an hotel for several days, folds the napkin and leaves it on the table beside the plate. Otherwise she should leave it scrumpled on the table and this rule also applies at dinner parties and luncheons where table napkins are used.

Children can be taught without too much prodding to sit straight in their chairs; to say 'Please' and 'Thank you' and to keep their mouths closed whilst eating; and not to talk or drink whilst they are masticating food. They will soon learn to pass things to each other if parents observe this courtesy themselves.

When children are old enough to use knives and forks, they can be taught to hold these implements correctly with the top of each shaft inside the palm, and the finger and thumb pressed gently along the handles for leverage. Adults often err here and can be seen gripping their knives and forks at the base like pencils with handles somewhere in the air.

There are a few simple and general conventions. Soup should be eaten quietly from the side of the spoon, and if it is necessary to tilt the plate slightly, this should be done away from the diner, not towards her. Bread must never be crumbled into the soup. Rolls are broken, never cut, each morsel broken off being small enough to be eaten in one piece. Transfer a portion of butter or jam from the butter dish or jam dish to the side-plate, and spread each morsel as needed. Bones are never picked except in the privacy of the home. Salt, if needed, should be poured in a small heap at the side of the plate, rather than sprinkled indiscriminately over the food. On pages 63–6 there is a section on the eating of special foods, and on pages 53–5 some notes on table-laying.

A guest should never attempt to retrieve dropped cutlery. In all probability the waiter or the host will have noticed the incident and will replace the implement without comment—otherwise ask quietly for a replacement. Never clatter knives and forks, or the spoon when stirring tea or coffee.

Conversation should generally be light, amusing and pleasant. Religion, health and politics are subjects best avoided on social occasions. The eating

50

pace should be neither too fast nor too slow—the diner should observe her neighbours and her hostess in order to finish at the right time. The meal cannot proceed until the most laggard eater has completed the course.

At the end of each course, used cutlery should be placed together on the plate, knives with cutting blade turned inward, forks with prongs uppermost, handles facing the diner. Spoons should be laid down with concave side uppermost. Put the soup spoon down on the under-plate if one is provided, rather than in the bowl.

Toasts

'The Queen'

At banquets and large formal dinners, 'The Queen' heads the list of loyal and patriotic toasts. This is always proposed by the chairman or the host and no reply is called for after the time-honoured words: 'Ladies and Gentlemen—The Queen!' Immediately after this speech which is proposed when the last course of the dinner is finished, the chairman or host will rise and announce: 'Ladies and Gentlemen, you may now smoke.'

Proposing and drinking a toast

Proposing a toast or making a speech can be an ordeal for those who are unaccustomed to the limelight and it may be helpful to bear in mind that social occasions call for toasts as opposed to speeches. At best they should be short, pithy and to the point. Economy of words, brevity of wit and absolute sincerity are the basic ingredients of a toast. The range is wide, covering loyal and patriotic toasts, civic toasts, church and school toasts, political and social toasts, sporting toasts and a miscellaneous collection of other toasts (wedding toasts are dealt with more fully on page 121). Each has its own background and humour and each requires separate treatment according to its case. Some research, a book of quotations and time are necessary in the preparation of any toast. The aspiring orator should study an appropriate book of speeches and toasts—they can be found in any library and most book shops—before he attempts to say his piece as from them he will learn to assess time and the number of words required for each toast and occasion.

If there is a toastmaster present, he calls upon the proposer, who rises. The proposer usually begins: 'Mr Chairman, Gentlemen', ('Ladies and Gentlemen') and concludes on the same note: 'Mr Chairman, Gentlemen, I now ask you to drink to ——' or 'I give you the toast to ——' or 'Ladies and Gentlemen, I ask you to join me in this salute to ——'. Immediately he has finished, everyone present, with the exception of the person to whom the toast is made (if present), raises his or her glass and takes a sip—only a sip as probably further toasts will be given and glasses are not always charged for each one. Usually people stand up for a toast though not always; the person who is toasted remains seated, and does not drink from his own glass.

Responding to a toast

Where the responder is the person whose health is toasted, he then rises and thanks the company for drinking his health and makes a brief speech.

Entertaining at Home

Formal dinner parties

Dinner parties are still the most important form of entertaining.

Invitations should be issued three weeks in advance of a formal dinner party (fourteen days prior to an informal one). All invitations should be answered within forty-eight hours. Where the invitation says *Black Tie,* men are expected to wear dinner jackets: otherwise dark city suits should be worn. In either case, women now wear evening dress—long skirts and pretty blouses for informal functions, and full-length dresses with attractive sleeves for formal occasions. If in doubt, a guest can telephone her hostess in order to find out what she herself will be wearing.

In a servantless household, guests should be greeted by the host in the hall, the men leaving their coats in the cloakroom and the women taking theirs upstairs to a bedroom which the host indicates—'The door on the left at the top of the stairs'—where clean towels and tissues should be at hand. If there are servants, the butler will direct the men, and the parlourmaid attend to the needs of the women before taking them downstairs to rejoin husbands waiting in the hall; the butler will then show the party into the drawing room. Women should precede their husbands when entering, the host and hostess being there to greet them and to make any introductions. Sherry, aperitifs or cocktails are then offered.

Laying a table is an art and an expression of personality, and no matter whether soft candlelight enhances gleaming silver on polished mahogany, or stainless steel is set on teak wood or plate glass, there is a challenge to be answered and an individual lay-out to be planned. A polished table cries out for lace mats over cork or asbestos, teak and plate glass for mats of modern design which offer protection and ornamentation.

A flower centrepiece affords richness and variety, but the inclination to buy  long-stemmed blooms for their beauty and elegance should be avoided or the guests may be hidden from one another. Bear in mind, too, that delicately coloured flowers which look lovely with the sun streaming across them often lose their impact under artificial light. Roses in low silver bowls: three dramatic flowers in an attractive container: floating flower-heads in a shallow salver—there is endless variety for those with colour sense and an artistic eye.

Cruets are not used at dinner, salts and peppers being placed conveniently round the table. Twenty-four inches (60 cm) should be allowed for each 'cover' if this is possible—twenty inches (50 cm) is the minimum space required for the comfort of each guest. Cutlery should be placed at the sides of each cover in order of use, working from the outside in, thus: on the right, the soup spoon, the meat knife and the pudding spoon, and on the left, the meat fork and the pudding fork. Although it is now sometimes called old-fashioned to place the pudding fork and spoon at the top of the cover, it is not incorrect. If butter is provided, though it rarely is at a dinner party, knives can be placed on the outside right, or between the soup spoon and the meat knife. Other cutlery is brought to the table as and when required. Knives should be laid with the blade turned inwards towards the plate, forks with the prongs uppermost. If you decide to place the pudding fork and spoon at the top of the cover, the spoon should be above the fork, with the prongs of the fork pointing to the right and the bowl of the spoon to the left. Glasses should be placed on the upper right of each cover, above the meat knife—they are used from the inside outwards. As it is now common practice to serve one or two all-purpose wines to accompany the entire dinner, only two glasses are usually provided. At a very formal dinner, port glasses are brought to the table when dessert is served. Table napkins can be placed on the side plate or on the place mat.

The good hostess chooses her guests carefully with an eye to the blending of their interests. Though she never dominates the conversation, she is able to steer it away from controversial topics which threaten to get out of hand. She will see no one guest hogs the conversation, and that the inarticulate, the diffident and the young are given a hearing when they struggle to contribute a point of view. By keeping abreast of national and international news, the good hostess will always have one or two opening gambits to spark off a fresh line of thought.

Every guest should realise that in accepting an invitation, an obligation is incurred to contribute something towards the success of the evening, whether it is charm of manner, wit or intelligence. The obligation extends to ensuring that attention is equally divided between partners to right and left.

At official and large important dinners, a strict rule of precedence is observed, the host taking the lady of highest rank in to dinner, the gentleman of highest rank escorting his hostess, and so on down the social scale. Within the ordinary household, it is now more usual for the hostess to enter the dining room with her most important female guest, the other women following behind, her husband in turn escorting the menfolk of the party. The seating plan should be worked out in advance, each woman sitting on the right of her dinner partner, although with a party of eight and a square table, the hostess must concede her place at the foot and sit on the left of her dinner partner.

Where a butler or parlourmaid is present in the dining room, soup is served from a tureen on the sideboard to each guest, commencing with the one on the right of the host, then the one on his left and so round the table irrespective of sex. All dishes are served from the left-hand side.

54

Without staff it is more convenient to serve a cold starter such as melon, prawn cocktail, paté, grapefruit or an avocado pear, as these can already be on the table when the guests enter the dining room.

Without staff, the main course should consist of something which can be kept piping hot. Joints and fowl can be carved in the kitchen and kept hot until required, the host serving these from the sideboard or the table. One vegetable—potatoes, for instance—can be dished up on the main serving dish with the meat or game, and a second vegetable, gravy and sauces can be passed round separately.

With staff, the upper servant serves the more important dishes, the under servant following with vegetables, gravy and sauces, standing on the left of each guest to serve and holding dishes in the left hand. Wine is served from the right-hand side. The single-handed hostess will probably find it more convenient to offer a cold third course as this can be placed on the table for guests to help themselves. A substantial main course can be followed by a light pudding, and every hostess has her secret store of special recipes for these occasions. With staff, hot or cold puddings or savouries can be served. If dessert is to follow, the table should be cleared of everything, except salt if nuts are included, and dessert plates brought in, the dishes being set on the table so that guests can help themselves.

Finger bowls are brought on the dessert plates at a formal dinner, these being removed with the accompanying d'oyley or under-saucer to the upper left of the cover so that fingers can be lightly dabbed in the water and patted dry on the table napkin. Port glasses are brought to the table with dessert, the decanter being first offered to the guest on the right of the host, then circulated clockwise round the table.

If a butler is present, he will serve the guests to the right and to the left of the host, and proceed clockwise round the table, returning to the host last. Servants leave the dining room when the port has been passed round once.

Whether coffee is served in the dining room or the drawing room largely depends on what is most convenient and practical for the hostess. Should she elect to leave the dining room, she will catch the eye of the most important female guest who will lead the way, the men rising and remaining standing until the host closes the door behind his wife. At this point it is for the hostess to ask whether any of her lady guests wish to go upstairs—on their return coffee will be served immediately.

In the dining room, the men group themselves round the host for general conversation, the port, and perhaps brandy, being passed round once more together with the cigars and cigarettes. Coffee is then served, the host indicating when it is time to join the ladies in the drawing room.

56

The accepted time to leave after a dinner party is 10.45 to 11.15, the most important guest making the first move. Very often the host will offer whiskey and soft drinks round 10.30 p.m. and this should be taken as a polite reminder that the party is drawing to a close. Guests should take leave of their host and hostess and perhaps those nearest to them, but departure should always be unobtrusive so as not to interrupt the conversation.

The young hostess

The young, inexperienced hostess giving her first dinner party should bear in mind that it is better to have three courses of good-quality food prepared and served well, rather than a six-course meal budgeted on the same time and money. Like all young wives without domestic help, she should pre-plan, laying the table, having glasses at hand—many wine merchants will lend what is required, only charging for breakages, and will also advise on appropriate wines—and clearing the kitchen to allow space for methodical stacking of dishes as they are brought from the dining room. Never apologise for any apparent limitations of china, silverware and so on; to do so is discourteous to your husband. Instead concentrate on a really charming flower centre-piece and soft lighting. Even when the dinner party is small and intimate, a quiet signal between the host and hostess can indicate when it is time for the women to retire from the dining room, thus giving the menfolk a short breathing space before they join their ladies in the drawing room.

The success of a dinner party depends to a large extent on the friendly blending of personalities and the happiness and enthusiasm of the young can often bring more joy to a dinner table than all the experience and sophistication of years.

A letter of thanks

Dear Mrs Birch,

A line to thank you for a lovely evening which my husband and I enjoyed enormously. What a delicious dinner you gave us and how beautiful your table looked! We arrived home feeling very happy, well fed and stimulated by pleasant company.

Again our warmest thanks,
Yours sincerely ——

Buffet suppers and drinks parties

A buffet supper is an excellent way of entertaining on informal lines, and here most of the preparations can be completed before the arrival of the first guests. The table should be arranged so as to encourage a one-way system of traffic with plates at the entrance end and cutlery at the exit end, food laid out attractively and with an eye to colour. Drinks can be served from a separate table, and bear in mind that although most people serve only a red and a white wine, it is quite correct to serve cider, soft drinks and beer. See that there are chairs enough and occasional tables and that the food is of a variety easily handled with a fork or fingers, although knives will be necessary in some instances and you should certainly provide a supply of small ones for buttering bread and rolls.

If help is available for the evening, see that it is on hand half an hour before the party starts, so that the assistant knows the lay-out of the kitchen and where is the best place for methodical stacking and drying of plates. She can hand round trays of drinks and food if cocktail eats are being served, remove and refill empty plates, and help with dish washing later. The hostess should see that guests mingle; that introductions are made where necessary; that diffident guests are absorbed into the party and that men do not congregate together in groups. Her job is to keep the party flowing and ensure that guests have an enjoyable evening.

Drinks parties can be run on the same lines although nothing more substantial than crisps, nuts and cheese biscuits need be served in the way of food. Make sure there are plenty of glasses and a supply of paper napkins with which to wipe up spills.

Luncheon parties

Luncheon parties at home follow a similar pattern to dinner parties although table decorations should be less elaborate. Invitations can be telephoned if the occasion is to be informal, or they can be hand-written or sent out on *At Home* cards a fortnight in advance of a formal party. The time, generally 1.00 or 1.30 p.m., should be stated clearly and guests should arrive punctually. A luncheon menu usually consists of three courses, followed by cheese and biscuits. Coffee and cigarettes can be served either in the dining room or the drawing room.

A buffet luncheon is a practical way of entertaining a number of guests when table space is limited.

Coffee mornings

Coffee mornings enable young wives to keep social contact with each other at times when they would otherwise be house-bound, and to offer a welcome to new-comers in similar circumstances. Invitations can be telephoned and a note sent to the new arrival asking her to come along at 11 a.m. The elderly, too, find this a pleasant and inexpensive way of keeping in touch with local friends. No elaborate preparations are necessary as only hot coffee, biscuits and pastries are served, and small talk—the exchange of everyday thoughts on everyday subjects—will usually roll happily along.

Entertaining Away from Home

Restaurant entertaining

Restaurant entertaining is a pleasant, if expensive, way of dispensing hospitality to family, friends, colleagues and business acquaintances.

When planning a restaurant party, the table should be booked in advance and the seating plan arranged as for a private party with the most important woman guest on the right of her host. The host should meet his guests a quarter of an hour before the time appointed for the meal in the cocktail lounge or foyer where he should offer drinks prior to leading the way into the restaurant. The head waiter will probably be around to direct the party to their table and each male guest should see his partner comfortably seated before sitting down himself.

It is a wise precaution for the host to decide the menu in advance, but if he prefers not to do so, he should suggest various dishes from the menu and guests making their choice should assume that not only does he know the restaurant well enough to do this with confidence, but also that these are the dishes that are within his means. All discussion in food, drink and service should be addressed to the host and never to the waiter. On bringing the wine, the waiter will first display the bottle unopened to the host and having received his signal of approval, will then uncork it and pour a little into the host's own glass. This the host will sip, and again if he approves it, will indicate with a slight nod and a polite 'thank you' that the waiter may now proceed to fill the rest of the glasses, starting with the woman guest on the right of the host. Liqueurs and brandy are offered after dinner, but are not essential after a luncheon, although they are often served at a business men's lunch.

If there is dancing in the restaurant, the host should first partner his most important woman guest, and the most important man should partner his hostess; on no account must any women be left to sit alone whilst others dance.

The party will usually break up around 11 or 11.30 p.m. and the host should see that all guests have transport home or are offered transport. In the event of a woman dining alone with a man, he will, of course, escort her home.

Theatre entertaining

Theatre entertaining can be arranged along the same lines, with a supper party before or after the show. Guests can meet at the home of the host and have a pre-theatre drink, or in the foyer of the theatre. Seating should be carefully

59

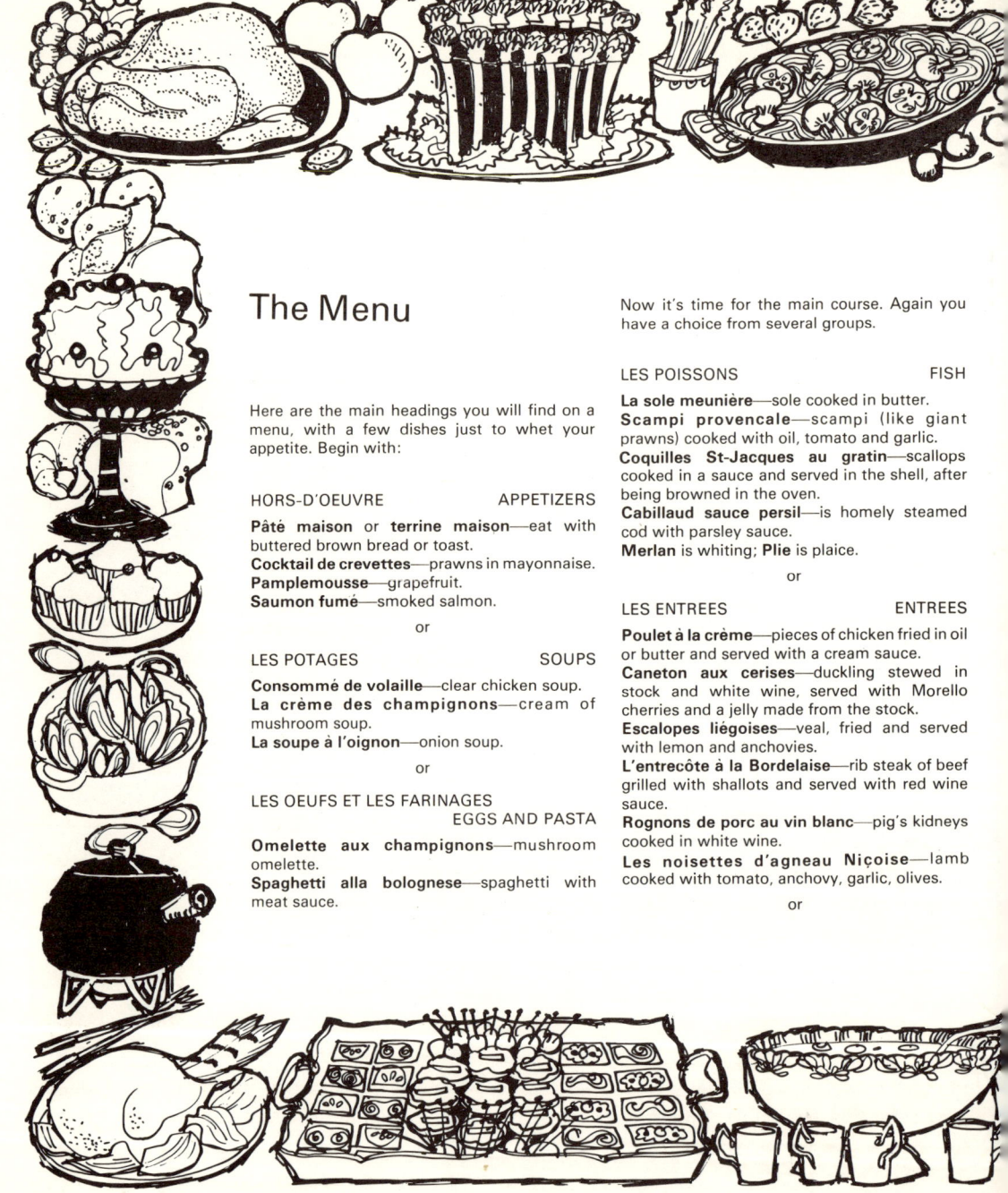

The Menu

Here are the main headings you will find on a menu, with a few dishes just to whet your appetite. Begin with:

HORS-D'OEUVRE   APPETIZERS

Pâté maison or **terrine maison**—eat with buttered brown bread or toast.
Cocktail de crevettes—prawns in mayonnaise.
Pamplemousse—grapefruit.
Saumon fumé—smoked salmon.

or

LES POTAGES   SOUPS

Consommé de volaille—clear chicken soup.
La crème des champignons—cream of mushroom soup.
La soupe à l'oignon—onion soup.

or

LES OEUFS ET LES FARINAGES
                    EGGS AND PASTA

Omelette aux champignons—mushroom omelette.
Spaghetti alla bolognese—spaghetti with meat sauce.

Now it's time for the main course. Again you have a choice from several groups.

LES POISSONS   FISH

La sole meunière—sole cooked in butter.
Scampi provencale—scampi (like giant prawns) cooked with oil, tomato and garlic.
Coquilles St-Jacques au gratin—scallops cooked in a sauce and served in the shell, after being browned in the oven.
Cabillaud sauce persil—is homely steamed cod with parsley sauce.
Merlan is whiting; **Plie** is plaice.

or

LES ENTREES   ENTREES

Poulet à la crème—pieces of chicken fried in oil or butter and served with a cream sauce.
Caneton aux cerises—duckling stewed in stock and white wine, served with Morello cherries and a jelly made from the stock.
Escalopes liégoises—veal, fried and served with lemon and anchovies.
L'entrecôte à la Bordelaise—rib steak of beef grilled with shallots and served with red wine sauce.
Rognons de porc au vin blanc—pig's kidneys cooked in white wine.
Les noisettes d'agneau Niçoise—lamb cooked with tomato, anchovy, garlic, olives.

or

LE BUFFET FROID   COLD TABLE

Here you will find cold meats, salads, lobster in mayonnaise and intriguing things in aspic jelly.

or

LA BROCHE
SPIT-ROASTED MEAT AND POULTRY

Chiefly poultry and game.

or

LES GRILLADES   GRILLS

Here many of the dishes have English names for they are nearly all chops or steaks.
Chop d'agneau—lamb chop.
Mixed grill.
Shish kebab—morsels of lamb, mushrooms, kidney, bacon, threaded on a skewer, grilled and served with a spicy sauce.

With your main dish you will want some vegetables or a salad:

LES LEGUMES   VEGETABLES

Haricots verts—French beans.
Epinards à la crème—spinach with fresh cream.
Petits pois à la francaise—green peas stewed in butter.
Asperges—asparagus.
Pommes de terre duchesse—mashed potato mixed with egg yolks and piped into pretty shapes.
Croquettes—the same mixture deep-fried.
Pommes de terre frites—chipped potatoes deep-fried.

LES SALADES   SALADS

Often people like a green salad—just lettuce with an oil and vinegar dressing—with a steak, or with the main course.

Now for a sweet or a savoury to finish with:

LES DESSERTS   PUDDINGS

Many of the puddings will be ice sundaes of one kind or another—*coupes*—or many-flavoured ice-cream—*bombes*—or delicious water-ices—*sorbets*—and there will usually be fruit salad and other dishes of fresh or cooked fruit with liqueur and cream.
Meringue glacée Chantilly—meringues sandwiched together with ice-cream and topped with whipped cream.
Soufflé tous liqueurs—a *souffle*—chiefly eggs and milk beaten up, filled with air, and baked till only the centre of the pudding remains liquid—flavoured with liqueurs.

or

LES CANAPÉS   SAVOURIES

A Welsh rarebit or anchovies on toast or something savoury of that kind can finish your meal, or you could have cheese or fresh fruit.

Coffee

The Wine list can be a poser to the uninitiated as a love and knowledge of good wine requires a long apprenticeship, best developed on, and if possible charged to, an expense account. It is fortunate that the expertise of wine waiters is always available to those who have the courage to ask for advice. The doubtful host, whether young or old, should never hesitate to seek help.

The following may be helpful:

1. Graves with hors d'oeuvre
2. Sherry with the soup
3. White burgundy or hock with the fish course
4. Red wine with the meat course
5. Champagne or sauternes with the pudding
6. Port with the dessert
7. Liqueurs with or after the coffee

Only at a very grand banquet or very formal dinner party are all these wines offered, and it is quite correct when dining out to provide only two, possibly a red and a white wine, or a choice of one or the other. It is a matter of taste and the state of the host's finances. A guest can always ask her host for a soft drink or a glass of water.

planned, and the host should pay for programmes and offer the first round of drinks during the interval. The second round should be paid for by a guest or guests, this being their only obligation on such an evening, apart from their cloak-room tip and their transport home.

Formal luncheons

Formal luncheons are ideal when women have to entertain guests in the course of their business, or professional lives. The time of the luncheon should be written in the bottom right-hand corner of the invitation card, *Luncheon 1 o'clock* and if it is organised for any specific purpose, this should be stated underneath the time: *To discuss our charitable aims for the coming year, To meet Lady Blankshire,* etc. Punctuality is imperative. A luncheon can consist of a sit-down meal of three or more courses, or it can be a buffet, in which case small tables each seating four or six guests can be arranged round the room, guests helping themselves to food before sitting down at the places allocated.

Women entertaining men in a business or professional capacity, find restaurant luncheons an ideal means of maintaining formality under semi-formal conditions. In this situation the menu should be first offered to the man and he should be asked to state his preference in regard to wine. Some women invariably find payment of the bill embarrassing, particularly if the waiter instinctively offers it to the man, but this can be overcome by the use of a credit card, or, where the same restaurant is used frequently, by having an arrangement with the management to sign the bill and pay later.

Special foods and how to eat them

ARTICHOKES   The leaves should be stripped off one by one, dipped in the accompanying sauce and conveyed to the mouth with the fingers. The white tip should be sucked dry and the rest of each leaf returned to the side of the plate. The heart is eaten with a knife and fork.

ASPARAGUS   When young and tender, this is often served as a separate dish with hot butter or sauce. Each stick is picked up by the stalk, dipped in the butter and conveyed to the mouth with the fingers. When served as a vegetable with meat or poultry, it is eaten with a knife and fork.

AVOCADO PEAR   The delicate flesh of the pear should be scooped gently from its case with a teaspoon. An oil and vinegar dressing is usually served.

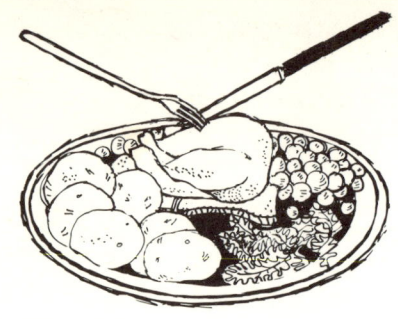

BIRDS Golden plovers, snipe, quails, and small pigeons are served whole—one to each guest. They are eaten with a knife and fork, the meat being cut from the breast and wings only. The legs are not eaten, nor should these small birds be turned over or dissected. With larger pigeons, half a bird is served to each person and only the wing and breast is eaten—this also applies to grouse and partridge.

CAVIAR   See paté

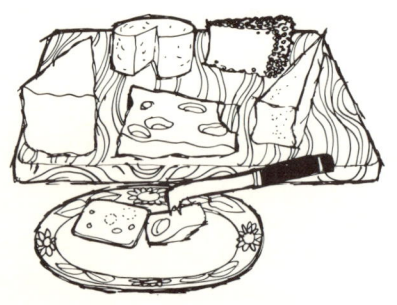

CHEESE   It is usual to cut a piece from the cheese on the cheese board, put this on the side plate, cut off small morsels as required, and put them on small biscuits or tiny pieces of bread with the knife provided. With Camembert, the gourmet will ensure that he eats the rind. This is permissible with other cheeses, but it is usually left at the side of the plate.

CHERRIES   Small stone fruit such as cherries, damsons, plums are eaten with a dessert spoon and fork, the spoon being raised to the lips to receive the stones which are then placed at the side of the plate.

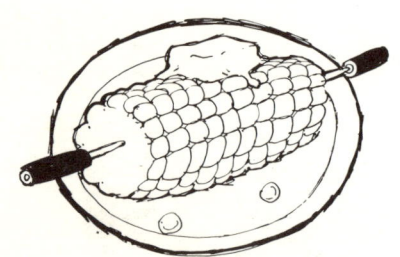

CORN-ON-THE-COB   A holder may be provided; if not, the cob is held in the fingers and eaten as tidily as possible, spreading the butter as required. If served as a vegetable, it is eaten in the same manner as peas.

GRAPEFRUIT   The fruit is halved across the sections, each half being placed in a bowl. The sections are cut carefully away from the skin and the fruit dredged with sugar. A few drops of liqueur adds flavour, a cherry provides decoration. Grapefruit can be iced or sprinkled with brown sugar and placed under the grill until the sugar melts. In either case, it is eaten with a teaspoon.

GRAPES   Snip off a small cluster with the scissors provided and eat singly. Remove pips and skin by placing the half-closed hand to the mouth and allowing them to fall into it, placing them at the side of the plate.

64

JACKET POTATOES   They should be halved and the potato scooped out with a fork, the jacket or skin being left at the side of the plate.

LOBSTER   Remove the flesh from the shell and cut it up with a small knife and fork, extracting the meat from the claws with a lobster pick.

MELON   The large water melon is seeded and eaten with a dessert knife and fork; cantaloupes are halved and eaten with a spoon; the small honeydew melon is eaten with a spoon or a dessert knife and fork. Ground ginger and caster sugar are usually served with melon.

OLIVES   If olives are part of an hors d'oeuvre, remove the stone with a fork; if they are served with drinks remove it discreetly with the fingers.

OYSTERS   Steady the shell on the plate with the left hand and, using the small fork provided, lever the oyster gently from the shell and eat it whole, savouring the flavour before swallowing. Cayenne pepper and thinly sliced brown bread and butter are served with oysters.

PATÉ or CAVIAR   These are eaten on small pieces of buttered bread or toast; use your knife to press the paté or caviar onto the toast, sprinkle with lemon if liked, and eat with the fingers.

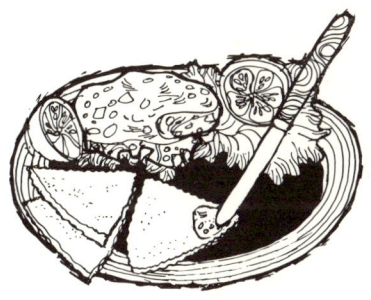

PEAS   Eat with a knife and fork, the prongs of the fork turned down.

PEACHES   Peel with a fruit knife, holding the fruit firmly on the plate with the fork. Remove the stone and then cut the flesh into pieces, eating with the knife and fork. Apples and pears are dealt with in the same way, except that they are quartered and the cores removed before eating.

PINEAPPLE   This is eaten with a knife and fork, a small piece at a time.

RAVIOLI   Eat with a fork.

SALAD When a salad is served on a small side plate, it should be eaten from this—not transferred to the main plate—with the same knife and fork as used for the meat, game or fowl being eaten.

SAVOURIES They are usually eaten with a fork only, but occasionally when necessary, a knife and fork are used.

SCALLOPS in the shell. Eat with a fork.

SNAILS They are generally served on the Continent with a small tweezer-like implement for holding, and a little lobster-pick type of fork for extracting the snail.

SOUP Drink from the side of the soup spoon, not the tip, without audible sound. For obvious reasons, if the soup plate has to be tilted, this should be at an angle away from the diner rather than towards him.

SPAGHETTI Twist a small amount around the fork and convey quickly to the mouth. Practice will make the diner adept in the art of managing wayward strands.

WHITEBAIT These tasty morsels must be eaten whole—head and eyes included. They are eaten with a fork, one or two at a time.

Parties and Anniversaries

Children's parties

Children's parties provide the young with their first social venture into other people's homes, and also with the opportunity of showing hospitality to friends in their own homes. The arrangements will naturally be made by the parents of the child and it is better to divide the age groups in large families so that they do not overlap too much. A party for three- to six-year-olds should be limited in numbers to not more than a dozen children; the seven-to-ten age group can include up to twenty guests if the home and the party room are large enough to take that number.

Children should be encouraged to write out their own invitations from an early age and these can take the form of a short hand-written letter, or be chosen from the many decorative invitation cards that are now on sale at all good stationary shops. If hand-written, they can be worded on the following lines:

Dear Emma Jane,

I shall be seven years old on Saturday, August the 17th and I should very much like you to come to my birthday party which will be from 4 to 7 p.m.

Will you let me know soon whether you can come?

Love from

Fiona

Mothers should see that replies are sent immediately—if possible hand-written by the child invited who will, of course, take a small present for her young hostess.

The room to be used for the party should be gaily decorated, perhaps with coloured streamers and balloons. There are now very pretty paper tablecloths in nursery designs with matching mugs and plates which are suitable for summer birthday parties held in the garden, otherwise the table can be laid with a coloured cloth and a general design built round it, the birthday cake having pride of place as a focal point.

Tea should be a sit-down affair beginning within half an hour of the guests' arrival. Small sandwiches of brown and white bread cut into triangles and filled with chopped dates and banana, salmon and cucumber, chopped hard-boiled eggs and tomato mixed with a little salad cream, ham or tongue—four varieties are sufficient, allowing three triangles for each child; malt and fruit loaf, tiny sausage rolls, iced biscuits or fairy cakes, jellies, fruit salad or a trifle—small helpings of not more than two of these; lastly the birthday cake, this being a sponge rather than a fruit cake, beautifully iced with the child's name upon it

and the appropriate number of candles, forming the *pièce de résistance,* to be cut as the children sing 'Happy Birthday' to their young hostess.

Milk, weak tea, orange and lemon squash, ginger beer, milk shakes, blackcurrant juice, are all ideal as party drinks. When the party is for very young children, buttered rusks, minute sandwiches filled with honey, mashed banana or egg, sponge fingers, fairy cakes and biscuits shaped as little men or animals, a home-made sandwich cake, and individual jellies topped with a whirl of cream provide all that is required.

Paper hats, crackers, and balloons can be distributed when tea is over and the entertainment about to begin.

A short spell of television, a Puppet Show or Punch and Judy, perhaps a ventriloquist entertainment of up to three-quarters of an hour, (look in your local paper for ideas), gives tummies time to settle down after the birthday tea, and this is the time to give visiting parents some refreshment or a much-needed drink. The table can be cleared and furniture moved for games, which must be chosen according to the age of the children; take care that with all age groups, a quiet game follows on a strenuous one. Hunt the Thimble, Hide and Seek, Musical Chairs, a Treasure Hunt, a Guessing Game, London Bridge and Sir Roger de Coverley are all popular with young people. Small prizes can be given to the winners: coloured pencils, crayons, a painting book, a pretty handkerchief, a plastic purse, and so on.

A quarter of an hour before the party ends, children can be given a soft drink and a biscuit or small cake, and they can then take a lucky dip into a bran tub, filled with paper shavings and hidden gifts. These need only be inexpensive trifles but they spell an exciting finish to a happy occasion.

Children should be taught to thank the mother and the young hostess of the party, and to say good-bye to them and the small guests.

Mothers who have left their offspring at the party, rather than staying for a cup of tea, should collect them promptly so that their small fry do not become anxious about being left behind when others have gone.

Small points to remember

An open fire should have a securely fixed guard and birthday candles should be shielded from draught. Fairy light bulbs get hot and should be beyond reach of small grasping hands. Tea-pots and containers of hot liquids should be placed where only adults have access to them. Excited young children 'forget' to ask for the lavatory and mothers or older children should escort them upstairs fairly frequently during the party. Have a face-cloth and towel at hand for sugary mouths and sticky fingers.

Coming-of-age parties

Coming-of-age celebrations can take many forms and it is now a matter of choice whether the eighteenth or the twenty-first birthday party draws friends and relations together. Often two parties are held: one for family, relations and friends with the father and mother acting as hosts; the other organised and run entirely by the young person concerned, the parents making a brief appearance as guests.

Whatever is decided upon, the venue of the party, the number of guests and the type of entertainment are important factors. A family celebration with a widely spaced age-range of guests calls for a sit-down meal with the birthday cake as the table's centre-piece, a few speeches and toasts, the first proposed by the fond father to the future of his offspring, glasses being charged in readiness for the high spot of the evening. Champagne or a sparkling wine is the usual drink, but soft drinks or cider can be served if preferred.

A buffet supper, followed by dancing, a private dance, a theatre party, a night club or discotheque—these are all popular ways in which the young like to celebrate their coming of age. But it must always be remembered that this is an occasion of great joy for the parents and they must never be left out or made to feel unwanted. The happiest solution is to have a family party, however small, and, circumstances permitting, a second celebration planned and financed by the celebrant.

Community centre party for the elderly

When organising a party for elderly people, there are several points which it is important to remember. Although the food should look attractive, it should not be too rich, otherwise delicate digestive systems may be upset. A good selection of food is advisable so that guests may take what they prefer, allowing for possible difficulties of diet. Try, for instance, to provide for diabetics. Any games which are organised should not be over-strenuous and should be interspaced with quiet periods when the elderly folk can sit around and talk amongst themselves, or perhaps have a cup of tea.

When the first guests arrive, they will probably be quite happy to sit and chat for a while until everyone is ready to commence the party in earnest. Ensure that everyone is introduced and that shy people are not isolated.

It is usual to begin the meal, whether 'sit-down' or buffet (the latter allows for plenty of choice, though it may be a strain for very elderly and frail guests, a point which should be watched) shortly after all the guests are present. If it is a Christmas occasion, crackers on the table are a 'must' as people of all ages enjoy these.

At such a party it is a great asset to have a piano and a good pianist who can set the mood for a sing-song by starting with numbers guaranteed to set people humming—for example, old songs which were popular when the guests were young. People may well commence singing spontaneously; otherwise, the organiser or the pianist can ask them all to join in. This should get the evening off to a good start—or be used to round off the entertainment at the end of the party.

Old-time dancing is popular with older folk who are still active and if the pianist is seeking a break, a record player could be brought into operation. Of course, a performer can be hired to entertain the guests, such as a ventriloquist, or a local singer. Details of performers can usually be found in local newspapers.

If this is a Christmas treat, the highlight of the evening should be a Christmas tree adorned with gifts: hankies, small bottles of eau-de-cologne, small boxes of chocolates, face tissues in gay wrappers, brooches, calendars, packets of cigarettes, book tokens, etc.

A small-scale treasure hunt would also fit in well with this type of party with, of course, written clues en route and a prize for the winner.

Finally, as a friendly gesture at the end of a warm and friendly evening, guests should be offered a snack and a drink before leaving, the organisers and committee seeing that everyone has transport.

Family occasions

There are various special occasions in a family's life, usually marking stages in the growing-up of the children, which may be celebrated with a small party for adults and children, relatives and friends. Buffet dishes are very useful on such occasions—savoury flans, sausage rolls, small sausages on sticks, little sandwiches, trifles, a simple sponge, a celebration cake. It is usual to provide tea or coffee, a selection of squashes for the children, and perhaps a light white wine for their elders. Such celebrations might mark a child's Confirmation, which in the Church of England usually takes place at the age of twelve or over, or Catholic First Communion, which takes place when a child is about eight. It is an honour to be invited to join a family on such an occasion. Guests should take a small gift for the child and should write a note of thanks to the hostess afterwards.

It is a particular honour to be asked to join a Jewish family for a boy's *Bar-Mitzva,* which marks his full assumption of religious responsibility, usually taking place on his thirteenth birthday or the Sabbath immediately following it. Men and women should wear hats for the synagogue ceremony, and should take a present for the boy to the joyous party which follows—preferably something which will indicate awareness of the fact that he is now growing into manhood. The Reform and Conservative movements have instituted the *Bas-Mitzva,* which is a parallel ceremony for girls.

70

Wedding anniversaries

A traditional list of wedding anniversaries is as follows:

1. **paper**	2. **cotton**	3. **leather**	4. **silk**	5. **wood**	6. **iron**
7. **copper or wool**		8. **bronze**	9. **pottery** 10. **tin**		11. **steel**
12. **linen**	13. **lace**	14. **ivory**	15. **crystal** 20. **china**		25. **silver**
30. **pearl**	35. **coral**	40. **ruby**	45. **sapphire**		50. **gold**
55. **emerald**		60. **diamond**			

It is pleasant to mark each anniversary with a gift made from the appropriate material. Opinions on the symbols for the lesser ones do vary, but on silver (the twenty-fifth), gold (the fiftieth) and diamond (the sixtieth) tradition is fixed. Suggestions for special celebrations of these great family occasions are given below. And if one is fortunate enough to celebrate seventy-five years of marriage, tradition allows a double-diamond affair.

A **silver wedding,** being something of an achievement in this day and age, calls for an announcement if only to proclaim to the world and younger members of society, that it is still possible to stay the course for a quarter of a century. A press notice sent in by the happy couple or their offspring on the following lines is the usual form:

> JONES—SMITH—On March 12 1949, at Christ Church Lancaster Gate, W.2., James M. Jones to Jane Smith. Present address: Petersfield House, Hallam Road, Eastbourne, Sussex.

There should be an exchange of gifts between the couple, and the family, perhaps pooling their resources, should endeavour to present a gift of silver to their parents. Other close friends, relations and small grand-children should give a present, no matter how modest.

The celebration may take any form: a drinks party, luncheon, dinner party or buffet. Invitations should be sent well in advance. You can use ordinary *At Home* cards, without mentioning the nature of the occasion to those outside the family circle and close friends, who will in any case know what is afoot, or you can have special *At Home* cards printed in silver, with the words *To celebrate our Silver Wedding* added. It is pleasant to give the bride a replica of her first bouquet. There should be a wedding cake trimmed with silver to grace the occasion, and this should be cut, as was its counterpart, by the bride, helped by her bridegroom of twenty-five years ago, while glasses are being charged with champagne or sparkling white wine for the toasts and speeches. These should be limited but happy, the eldest son proposing the first 'To the health and happiness of our dear parents' on behalf of the family. The husband should reply to this on behalf of his wife and himself. The second toast is proposed by

the best man if he is present, and others couched in a reminiscent vein can follow if desired. The husband, in replying to the toasts, should not forget to give his wife due credit for the happiness and stability of the marriage; the eldest son should be at pains to thank both parents for a happy childhood and the advantages he has reaped from their sound upbringing and loving care. Such things are left unsaid for most of a life-time and this is an occasion when the heart can speak openly, and should.

Room and table decoration would look pretty in white and silver. The eldest son should sit next to his mother, the eldest daughter next to her father, other members of the family and grandchildren ranging themselves alongside. If there is dancing, the husband leads the first dance with his wife, her eldest son and the best man claiming her next as partners.

A **golden wedding** is the 'grand' landmark in a family history and an occasion for celebration and quiet content. The bride and bridegroom of fifty years may yet be hale and hearty, but the anniversary arrangements are usually organised by the eldest son in consultation with other members of the family. The press announcement should be on the same line as that for the silver wedding, with an adjustment to the date, of course. Presents should be gold if possible, though small, as by now the couple will have acquired all the wordly possessions they require and gifts should be a token of love and esteem, rather than for practical purposes. A small brooch, a pill box, a golden commemoration spoon from the older members of the family, yellow flowers from friends, golden wine or spirits, champagne, amber-coloured glass, roses for the garden, yellow pottery or breakfast ware, small yellow posies from great-grandchildren; perhaps records, a radio or even a colour television from more affluent members of the family, indeed anything in the way of small luxuries which will make for the comfort and entertainment of the couple.

The party may be celebrated in an hotel or restaurant and as many of the original wedding guests as possible invited, together with grand-children and great-grand-children. No formal invitations are issued, the older members of the family writing personal letters to all those whose presence will give pleasure to their parents. Again there will be a wedding cake, this time decorated in gold. Dress on this occasion is usually informal, as are speeches after the cutting of the cake. The husband may be quite happy to reply to the toast, but he can delegate this pleasant duty to his youngest grandson if he so wishes. There is no need for planned entertainment to follow the dinner as no doubt all the elderly guests will be content to reminisce as they drink their coffee and smoke. When the couple begin to show signs of fatigue, the party should be brought to a close by the eldest son, who should then see his parents safely home.

The Diamond Wedding is another landmark in the history of the family and it is on this occasion, the sixtieth anniversary, that a royal congratulatory telegram may be requested. Application should be made by a member of the family or a friend about a month in advance of the anniversary date, and should be accompanied by the original marriage certificate, or a copy of it (obtainable as described on page 151; send details of the date and place of the wedding, the groom's full name, and the bride's full maiden name). This certificate will be returned to the sender. The letter should be sent to The Assistant Private Secretary to Her Majesty the Queen, Buckingham Palace, London, S.W.1. The word ANNIVERSARY should be written in the bottom left-hand corner of the envelope.

The party is usually a quiet affair confined to members of the family, but if any of the original guests are fit and well enough to attend they must be given a splendid welcome. The anniversary cake and the food should be fairly plain, and the whole celebration planned according to the health and stamina of the now aged couple. Flowers, presents and good wishes arrive early in the day and the party should be brought tactfully to an end directly the central figures begin to show signs of weariness.

A hundredth birthday—and over
A hundredth birthday is a magnificent achievement and should be marked by cards, greetings telegrams, flowers, and if possible, a gathering of close friends and relatives. On this occasion too a royal congratulatory telegram may be requested. A member of the family or a friend should apply about a month before the birthday, writing to The Assistant Private Secretary to Her Majesty The Queen, Buckingham Palace, London, S.W.1., with the words *HUNDREDTH BIRTHDAY* written in the bottom left-hand corner of the envelope. The original birth certificate, or a copy of it, should be enclosed. Copies may be obtained as described on page 151; an enquirer should send details of the full name, the date and place of birth, and the names of the parents.

If the family would like to see a report in the local paper, they should contact the News Editor a week or so in advance. He will usually be happy to send a reporter and a photographer along on the day.

Royal congratulatory telegrams are also sent on the 105th birthday, and on subsequent birthdays. The same procedure should be followed.

A Weekend Visit

The good hostess inviting friends to stay will find it better to write rather than telephone, as this obviates the possibility of misunderstanding the date and duration of the proposed visit. A week-end implies from Friday to Sunday night unless otherwise stated and this can be stressed by suggesting train arrival and departure times on those days, or giving the guests a convenient time of arrival if they are travelling by road.

The good hostess will see that the bed-linen is well-aired and rooms comfortably warm for her guests, with extra blankets at hand for chilly people and extra pillows. Bedside lights and electric fires should be checked beforehand to ensure they are safe and in good working order. Wardrobe space, a supply of coat-hangers and empty drawers lined with fresh paper should be made available, and soap and towels laid out in readiness. The hostess wishing to cosset her guests will add those extra touches which show thought and loving regard: flowers on the dressing table, tissues, hair grips and aspirin in the drawer, a carafe of water and an air-tight tin of biscuits on the bedside table, together with a few books and magazines. A small supply of writing paper and stamped envelopes can be provided as a rescue operation for careless guests who leave theirs behind. If possible, extra newspapers should be ordered so that the guests have breakfast-time reading while the hostess is busy elsewhere.

In the wake of a warm welcome, guests should be taken to their rooms and shown the bathroom, the hostess mentioning at what time it will be at their disposal morning and evening. They can then be left to change and freshen up prior to joining their hosts for a drink before dinner. Any special entertainment planned for the weekend should have been mentioned in the invitation so that guests come suitably equipped, but the programme can be fairly flexible thus allowing some freedom of action, the main object being not to stifle them with over-attention nor yet neglect them. If town or city friends are snatching a brief respite in the country, they may be content simply to relax, and to enjoy a small intimate dinner party on the Saturday evening and meet a few friends of their hosts over drinks at noon on Sunday, or vice versa. If they are from the country, a theatre party and a dinner out on the town would provide a stimulating change. Hostesses with limited help—or none at all—should plan modestly on a scale that can be contained. To do otherwise is to risk domestic machinery grinding to a halt at a critical moment, and it is far better for guests to meet a few congenial friends at a well-organised, manageable luncheon than to witness an over-ambitious dinner party which flops miserably through lack of support in the wings.

74

The single-handed hostess entertaining lone women guests may find it convenient to serve a continental breakfast in bed, thus leaving herself a clear field downstairs to attend to necessary chores. She is not compelled to offer early morning tea nowadays and few people expect it. With a mixed party, it is better to serve breakfast in the dining room so that guests can help themselves to hot dishes from the sideboard: 9 a.m. is a reasonable hour to suggest for breakfast as few men care to lie in bed late.

Where there are children or babies in the party, a thoughtful hostess will see that washing and drying facilities are laid on, and provision made for the heating and cleaning of bottles. Every effort should be made to see that the mother can keep to the normal routine of their day so that they do not become fractious and so disrupt the harmony of the household and spoil the brief change the young parents hope to enjoy.

The good hostess will ensure that her good-byes are as warm as were her greetings, and that her guests leave her home at least a degree happier than when they entered it.

The appreciative guest will reply to all invitations promptly and in writing, mentioning the date, time and duration as set down, and letting the sender know how she proposes to travel and whether she can arrive at the suggested time. She will then endeavour to be punctual. Those invited to stay with elderly friends or in homes where there is no domestic help, should take only such luggage as can be handled personally without expectation of assistance. Greetings should be cordial and, according to the degree of intimacy, the guest will then adapt herself to the ways of the household and give tactful help where and as acceptable to her hostess, always bearing in mind that while she may find it embarrassing to sit in idleness, a hostess often finds it quicker and more convenient to 'go it alone', especially where there is a small kitchen. On the same premise, when a guest is offered breakfast in bed, this should be accepted with thanks and a smile. The general rule today is that in the absence of servants, a guest will make her own bed and keep her room tidy. She will also see that having bathed, she leaves the bathroom scrupulously clean and tidy.

A considerate guest will see that she packs everything she can possibly need for her stay: toothpaste, writing paper, envelopes and stamps, a book, needlework or knitting with which to occupy herself when her hostess is engaged elsewhere. She will also be punctilious in paying for telephone calls. As a token of appreciation—though this is not obligatory—she may like to bring her hostess a carefully chosen gift: candies, fruit, flowers, home-made jam, chocolates, a book or a record, and if there are children in the household, sweets or small toys. A man who likes his evening drink will not usually cause offence by a gift of wine or spirits to his host, so long as the bottle is presented tactfully.

On all occasions when entertainment is planned with the pleasure of the guest in mind, she should show her appreciation by entering whole-heartedly into the spirit of the event and rendering something towards its success.

In a one-servant household, a guest may expect to find her bed turned down at night and night clothes and dressing gown laid out, but she must unpack her own cases and make her own bed except on the morning of departure. She should not forget to tip the housemaid, and the cook if there is one, (page 88) with a word of thanks. She should never ring for, or give orders to, servants unless invited to do so by her hostess. On no account must she ask them to do her personal laundry or run errands.

The considerate guest will not forget that entertaining, even on a modest scale, is an expensive undertaking nowadays, and she will thank her hostess warmly for her stay before leaving and, most important, follow this up with a letter of thanks the following day, mentioning the highlights of her visit and the excellent food and care she has received. The letter should be hand-written.

A guest who has not given her hostess a small gift on arrival, may like to send flowers after her return home. This can be done through INTERFLORA, or arranged with a florist in the locality before leaving. Small cards are supplied and appropriate messages can be added or relayed as directed. But even so, a proper letter of thanks must be sent.

My dear Annabelle,

I have just unpacked and feel I must write at once to thank you for the lovely weekend. It was so marvellous to see you again and to find you happily installed in your new cottage, which I think is charming and full of character. It is so nice, too, that you have good neighbours, all of whom I enjoyed meeting. I am sure you are going to love country life after so many busy years in Town and I shall look forward to seeing you often—as often as you like to invite me! Don't forget, however, that I have a spare room and can accommodate you happily whenever you can tear yourself away.

Again my warmest thanks for everything—what a good cook you are!

Affectionately ——

Clothes

Women's dress

The desire to look attractive is an inborn characteristic of every woman and the degree of time and trouble she is prepared to spend on achieving a good appearance is indicative of her status and self-pride. The end result bears little relation to the price tag of her clothes as the most inexpensive garment worn with casual elegance can draw more admiration than couture fashion on someone careless of good grooming and personal freshness, which operation begins in the bath, proceeds with a good deodorant, a clean bra, unwrinkled tights, unrimmed finger nails, shining hair and well-pressed clothes.

Hats are still important and should be worn for weddings, funerals and christenings—indeed all church functions. Royal Ascot is the occasion for large hats; royal garden parties, official luncheons, women's luncheons, both social and professional, and civic functions, for small ones. Elderly women with pretty hair look charming in tulle and veiling hats and for any woman whose hair is not her crowning glory, a brimmed hat provides a pleasing frame for her face.

Gloves are a must for the bride's mother receiving her guests at a wedding reception, and it is correct to wear them at official functions and luncheon parties of a formal nature. Long gloves are still worn at grand banquets, although they are now always removed entirely when the meal commences. It is no longer fashionable to slip one's hand out of the glove and tuck the finger-parts in the glove-sleeve; they should be laid across the knees or put beside or inside the evening pochette while eating.

Country gloves should be of leather in plain dark colours, or string in beige or yellow. White washable gloves are correct with summer dresses. Women always shake hands with their gloves on—men always remove them.

Long dresses are now worn both in town and country for most functions—warm woollen long-sleeved dresses for evening, long skirts and elegant Edwardian high-necked blouses for 6 o'clock drinks and pretty Laura-Ashley-type dresses for both day and evening wear are worn by the young everywhere.

Business and office dresses should be decorous, but most girls who have an attractive figure like to reveal as much of it as possible. Fashion is a transient quantity—the paradox being that whereas working gear now reveals all, evening wear is strictly cover-up. Until a few years ago, the reverse applied.

Men's evening dress

For important banquets and very formal occasions, men wear what is often spoken of as 'white tie and tails'. This consists of a black tail coat with silk lapels, black trousers, white waistcoat, stiff-fronted white shirt, white wing collar and a white bow tie.

For small dances, dinner parties and less formal evening occasions, men wear what is usually known as a 'dinner jacket', which consists of a black jacket with silk lapels but without tails, black trousers, waistcoat or cummerbund, plain or pleated white or coloured shirt, and a black or coloured silk or velvet bow tie. The dinner jacket can be single or double breasted, is normally made in barathea, mohair or velvet and can be in a rich dark colour instead of in black. With either outfit, black patent leather, laced or elastic-sided shoes should be worn. Black pumps are unusual today.

Men's morning dress

While black morning coats with grey or lavender waistcoats and striped trousers continue to be popular and correct for weddings and other functions where morning dress is required, Moss Bros say the new trend is the grey morning suit which consists of a grey coat with grey matching trousers and waistcoat. They get little demand for velvet suits for weddings, but these are sometimes worn for evening functions. The accessories with morning suits used to be only white shirt, white stiff collar (wing or turned down), and grey tie, but now pastel shades are creeping in for shirts (collar attached) and ties, and look particularly well with the all-grey morning suits.

Wardrobe for hire

Economics and lack of space limits every woman's wardrobe today, and while she may be fully equipped to meet the ordinary demands of her business and social life, there are those occasions which cry out for the Midas touch which is beyond her purse. The sensible woman will not be slow to seize upon the practical advantages of hiring these luxury items when the need is rare and the function all-important: furs, jewels and couture fashion at a fraction of the purchase price; sporting clothes and equipment—for men as well as women—ski and apres-ski wear, sailing clothes, highland dress, riding kit and saddlery, and lastly, for that once-in-a-lifetime traditional wedding, a dreamy gown of fabulous romantic splendour. This Cinderella service is in active operation and available to all.

Messrs Moss Bros, whose address is given on page 153, are renowned for the speed and efficiency of their clothes-hire service and know-how on what is the correct dress for every social, professional and sporting occasion. They have branches throughout the country (listed on page 153) and extensive London show-rooms where a bride, bridegroom, parents and entire retinue can be fully equipped within an hour. As a preliminary, send for a fully illustrated Bridal

Folder. No deposit is required—only proof of identity. All prices include V.A.T.; an idea of the present (1974) price range is given on page 153. Packing and carriage add a small sum to the cost of hire. In addition to wedding gowns, there is a fine selection of tiaras and head-dresses (the latter for sale only), bridesmaids' dresses, kilts, uniforms and pages' outfits.

Furs are insured by Messrs Moss Bros whilst in the customer's possession except when taken out of the British Isles. They are not covered for return transit and therefore, if they cannot be returned personally, they should be sent by post insured to their full value. Bankers' or store references are taken up or a suitable deposit is required. Up-to-the-minute fur jackets, coats and stoles in mint-fresh condition are always available, and some sample prices are given on page 153. Send for a fully illustrated Fur Folder. The hire charge is based on the assumption that the customer returns them on the first business day after they are worn. And, incidentally, if a customer decides to buy the fur she has hired, the hire fee is deducted from the purchase price.

Ski-wear. Help and advice from Moss Bros ensure that clients are warmly, comfortably and correctly dressed at all times during their ski holiday. Hire bookings for winter holidays up to mid-January begin in August and they advise early bookings for the widest possible choice. Payment of the hire fee reserves the outfit and if afterwards a customer decides to buy it, the full fee will be credited to the purchase. A very comprehensive folder is available in colour, but customers should call at Covent Garden to see an even wider range of styles and colours. Although their many branches carry only a small selection of ski-wear, they are quite happy to order a certain style from Covent Garden, or even a selection for you to choose from. No deposit is required—only proof of identity. Outfits are sent well before the holiday date to avoid delay during the Christmas period. Goods are hired to customers on the understanding that they shall be returned in undamaged condition and customers are responsible for them at their current selling value until they are returned.

Riding. Leather boots can be hired, for one day or longer as required; clothing, saddles, whips, hats, etc., are for hire at a negotiable price, but roughly half the selling price or less if customer's requirements can be met from re-conditioned stock.

Underwater equipment and water skis. Wet suits for diving or sailing can be hired for a weekend; water skis; a snorkel (face mask and fins inclusive); a life jacket; sailing jacket and trousers. An aqualung, underwater camera, harpoon gun, diver's knife, depth gauge—all these items are there to choose from. A deposit to the full value of these goods will be required. Write to Moss Bros for the leaflet.

Cameo Corner, whose address is given on page 153 and who can supply fine

antique and modern jewellery to add the final touch of glitter to any evening, base their terms of 10% (per day) on the value of the article with a moderate minimum charge and a deposit for the full value, the hirer being responsible for insurance cover during the time that articles are in her possession. There is experienced help to guide customers' choice for any dress or function, whether the magic lies in diamonds, pearls, emeralds, rubies, sapphires, onyx, amethyst or turquoise. Write, or better still, call.

Young's Dress Hire (address on page 153) specialise in bridal and evening wear and can supply a complete outfit with shoes, bag and gloves for each occasion. No deposit is required but bankers' or store references are taken up and the customer must take out insurance cover for the period of hire and register each item to its full value for the return journey. It is worth-while writing for details.

Decorations

Orders, miniature decorations and medals are worn with evening dress when members of the Royal Family are present. They are also worn at official banquets and receptions, at naval and military dinners, entertainments given by a Lord Lieutenant within his county, and at functions given by Cabinet Ministers, Lord Mayors and Mayors.

Travel Etiquette at Home and Abroad

In today's shrinking world, people go further and faster, and whether travel is for pleasure or profit, whether the journey is ten miles or ten thousand, whether the means of transportation is coach, train, ship or plane, each person so engaged is for a time dependent to some extent upon the whims and inclinations of fellow travellers. And in this juxtaposition, common courtesy and consideration are vital to co-existence.

Rail travel

Rail travel is still the most convenient and widely used means of public transport for the general public, though it does demand from its subscribers the triple virtues of patience, hope and fortitude. Having attained this state of grace, the object of ordinary men and women is to pay a legitimate fare and proceed on their lawful occasions without let or hindrance and it is a pity that the odds are so often stacked against their doing just that.

Petty irritations can be avoided by the exercise of good manners and consideration for others. Don't be an aggressive traveller; do ask permission of those already established in the carriage before opening or closing windows; don't fill up passenger seats with luggage and personal items in a crowded train; do collect up paper bags and orange peel if it is necessary to eat in the carriage en route; don't discuss intimate relationships in a manner likely to embarrass the more restrained; do provide books, drawing materials and quiet games for children making long journeys; don't smoke in non-smoking compartments; do be pleasant and friendly. Travel should be a happy experience—all too often it is a nightmare.

Bus travel

Bus travel calls for tolerance, agility and stamina, and a few old-fashioned courtesies such as giving up seats to pregnant women and the elderly, and helping young mums who, with one pair of hands are dealing with babies, toddlers, folding prams and heavy shopping at the same time. Men who are escorting women should see them safely on the bus before boarding themselves and alight first in order to help them off. It is bad manners to harangue drivers for delays due to traffic congestion. Conductors are often rude, abusive or truculent—they are just as often subjected to the same treatment. Both sides should cool it—they are interdependent upon each other's good-will.

Coach travel

Coach travel is an economical and deservedly popular means of inter-city journeying, but it does entail close contact with fellow beings and renders each vulnerable to the other. Travel agencies can ensure that tickets equate with places available, but they cannot dictate that passengers shall be congenial. Usually they are and whether because of, or in spite of, the intimate nature of this type of travel, seat neighbours do respect each other's limited privacy, and by unspoken consent observe those courtesies and conventions which make for pleasant travelling. Only small luggage can be taken inside the coach and a head-rack is provided for this—the two larger cases allowed can be stowed away in  the outside rear compartment of the coach by the driver, so there is no problem of gangways being blocked and, since there are regular stops for food and exercise, it is unnecessary to scatter orange peel, crumbs and paper bags indiscriminately or fidget about to the annoyance of a dozing neighbour. Most long distance coaches possess their own system of air conditioning, which saves a fuss over the opening and closing of windows. Heavy smokers should always appreciate that the habit may be obnoxious to others and can cause real physical distress to an asthmatic or otherwise afflicted person in an enclosed area. Formal introductions are unnecessary on coach journeys and light conversation helps to pass the time agreeably. Always say 'Goodbye' to an immediate neighbour when leaving a coach, and on reaching the final destination thank the driver for a safe journey, at the same time handing to him a modest tip.

Coach tour operators generally issue their own brochures which contain booking forms and itineraries, plus guidance on the amount of luggage which can be accommodated for each passenger. As this is limited, it is wise to pack drip-dry, crease-resistant articles of clothing and travel in a warm but lightweight woollen coat. On this type of holiday, small groups of people are living at close quarters for periods of ten to fifteen days, and if a pleasant atmosphere is to prevail throughout the trip, good manners are essential. Some firms allocate seats on a 'first come first served' basis when the booking is made, and on this premise a late booking is an acceptance of that condition and in effect an assurance that there will be no grumbling if seats are not positioned advantageously. Other firms see that passengers change their location inside the coach with every leg of the tour. Only in rare instances is there complete freedom of choice, but should this be so, it is to be remembered that front seats are considered the prime position and they should not be hogged by a few selfish people throughout the tour. Nightly hotel accommodation is pre-arranged by the coach tour companies and some form of evening entertainment laid on—sometimes a visit to the local theatre, sometimes a dance. It is polite for tourists to join in any entertainment and to help in making the social side of the tour a success. As an early morning start is necessary where a great deal of ground has to be covered each day, passengers must be downstairs at the prescribed time, and it is exasperating to the entire party if a few people are consistently late for breakfast. Before leaving the hotel, tourists should see that bedrooms are tidy, and hotel property intact. Coach tour bookings are inclusive of gratuities and only where special services have been given need they be offered. It is customary, however, to make a collection for the driver on the last day of the tour.

Air travel

Air travel is invariably booked in advance and as planes run ideally to a tight schedule, in spite of the inevitable delays, punctuality is important. Passengers should reach the air terminal at the specified time—especially if the airport is at some distance from the terminal and taxis elusive and prohibitive in cost. Jets cannot and do not wait for late-comers. Baggage is weighed and registered by the stewards when you 'check in' at the airline's desk at the airport, and for convenience of passengers on long-distance flights is often labelled *REQUIRED AT NIGHT STOPS* and *NOT REQUIRED ON JOURNEY*. The small flight bag permitted inside the plane should contain necessary toilet articles, a comfortable pair of slippers, reading matter and anti-glare sun glasses. Package travel obviates the rush for seats on boarding the plane as tour planes are usually chartered and seat numbers assigned, but the independent traveller not holding a first class ticket is often subjected to a 'free for all' in her effort to get aboard and find a place, and the most unlikely people contribute to these appalling displays of bad manners. A well-mannered air passenger is considerate of staff and fellow-travellers, neither talking too much, smoking too much nor drinking too much. In a rarified atmosphere each one of these habits is tiresome—together they are intolerable. Newspapers should be kept folded whilst being read, not spread out in full so that companion passengers are overwhelmed with flapping pages. Try to avoid to-ing and fro-ing during the flight at times when seat companions may wish to sleep. Air hostesses are capable young people who ensure passengers' comfort and exude confidence and goodwill. Many of the girls, especially those from the East, have exquisite manners and are worth watching and emulating. Should the aircraft run into storm or temporary trouble, passengers should try to match their calm, and follow instructions as they are given. On landing, air staff usually stand at the entrance of the plane to wish their passengers goodbye. They should be thanked warmly for a safe and pleasant flight. Apart from the luggage porters, air-line staff are never tipped.

Etiquette at sea

At sea, etiquette is casually informal, especially in the high season when travel companies offer the holiday-maker package cruises covering a whole new range of experience and exploration at an incredibly modest cost, so attracting a wide cross-section of the general public. This is big business and competitive, and each firm promoting this type of travel realises that the broader the horizon and the greater the comfort, the more far-reaching will be the demand. Having won their customers, they make every effort to ensure that from the moment of embarkation, the passenger is put at ease and that a relaxed social atmosphere rules the waves.

But even informality has its limits and a few unspoken courtesies must be observed if a pleasant life-style is to prevail during these brief encounters. Cabin accommodation is restricted and each occupant should respect the other's privacy and square yard of space. Each should use her own bunk for unpacking and share equally the amenities provided. There must be some agreement about the use of the shower and consideration between early and late bedders, toleration being the watch-word. Tidiness is essential. Large sums of money and jewellery should not be left lying about the cabin—the Purser will be happy to hold valuables in his office.

On short cruises an invitation to dine at the Captain's table is a compliment and should be accepted. On longer voyages such invitations are usually extended to distinguished passengers and may be for a single meal or for the whole passage. Introductions are made as they would be in a private house. A ship's dining room is run in the manner of a good hotel or restaurant and the Purser or the Chief Dining-room Steward is responsible for the seating list. Orders for wine should be given to the wine steward. It is inevitable that many of those sharing tables are strangers to one another and initial civilities may be a little strained, but if each tries to be pleasant and friendly without being intrusive, a congenial atmosphere should soon develop.

After the first night out, passengers change for dinner as they would at an hotel—the long cotton dresses at present so fashionably pretty are ideal, especially for after-dinner dancing. Social activities form a vital part of life aboard ship and a full programme of sports and concerts is usually organised by entertainment committees drawn from the passenger list. It is good manners to enter into the spirit of all festivities and to contribute something towards the success of each function.

Everyone with even a modest talent in any field should be prepared to help to entertain, and show their appreciation when entertained themselves.

When shore excursions take place, passengers should remain with their party as far as possible or at least be at the pre-arranged rallying point in good time to return to the ship.

On short cruises it is impolite to hold deck chairs for long periods by leaving books, magazines or bathing towels on them. On long sea voyages, it is permissible to arrange with the deck steward to 'hold' a deck chair during the entire trip and in this case it is accepted that a passenger's cushions, books, etc., can be left there without interference.

Passengers should never go on to the Bridge without the permission of the Captain or Officer in command, nor should they engage on-duty officers or crew in conversation.

Passengers in need of advice should consult the Cruise Director, the hostess or the Purser. Stewards and stewardesses attend to sea-sick passengers—they will call the doctor in case of emergency or when illness is serious enough to prevent passengers attending the surgery at the specified hours.

On a long sea trip, friendships flourish easily and languish quickly. It is a matter of personal inclination whether they are ratified at the end of a voyage. There is no social obligation to further a shipboard acquaintance and there is no cause for either side to take umbrage if *au revoir* proves to be goodbye. Even so, farewells should be warm and cordial so that no jarring note mars the close of a brief harmony and a memorable holiday.

Staying in an hotel

Hotel reservations should be made as far in advance as possible, preferably in writing. The letter should state clearly the number of rooms required, whether single or double, and if the latter, whether twin-bedded or otherwise, and for what period. Ask for a brochure or for terms and if these are satisfactory, confirm the booking and give an approximate time of arrival. If a booking is made by telephone, a letter of confirmation should reach the hotel within three days as with accommodation in short supply, proprietors cannot guarantee to hold rooms.

Signing the register is a simple but necessary procedure. On arrival a guest should make her way to the reception desk and give her name. She will then be asked to sign the Register. In this she should enter her status, her Christian name or initials, her surname—*Mrs. H. James, Miss Emma B. Jones*—and her permanent address. A married man accompanied by his wife signs on her behalf as well: *Mr. and Mrs. T. F. Brown, Captain and Mrs. Green, Sir John and Lady White.* When a married man or a bachelor travels alone, only the Christian name or initials appear with the surname: *John T. Brown, B. N. Right.*

On receiving the key and being shown to her room, the guest should ascertain what fire precautions are operable in the hotel; what type of escapes are provided and where these lie in relation to her own apartment. The elderly and

infirm should not accept accommodation which might prove hazardous in emergency and those with young children should make sure that rooms with barred windows have an exit other than a single staircase outside the door. This is not strictly speaking 'etiquette', but hotel managements have an obligation towards guests over and above supplying excellent food and comfortable beds, and a guest has a legitimate complaint if fire-fighting equipment is inadequate or obsolete—in registering it, she may not only be protecting her own life but the lives of others, and, in the long run, the reputation of the hotel and its management.

Hotel keepers quite rightly do not accept responsibility for money or valuables left by guests in bedrooms or public rooms and these things should be taken to the cashier, and a receipt obtained, as soon as possible after arrival so that they can be deposited in the hotel safe.

Dressing for dinner is unnecessary the first night of arrival and this gives guests an opportunity to observe the degree of formality accepted in regard to evening dress. So much depends upon the type of hotel, the time of the year and the clientèle. The large, fashionable hotels cater for the formal and the informal diner, the small comfortable residential hotels devoted to the comfort of elderly guests seem to have effected a happy compromise whereby residents 'change' and manage to look elegant without wearing full length dresses. The young subscribe whole-heartedly to the long Laura-Ashley-type of dress for day and evening wear and can be seen in resort hotel dining rooms everywhere. Country hotel clients seem to favour long skirts in silk or wool worn with Victorian blouses.

Introductions are usually informal during a stay in an hotel, except in the case of large cosmopolitan establishments where a relaxation from formality may be an invitation to exploitation. In smaller hotels it is courteous to smile and greet fellow-guests once they are known by sight. The degree of friendliness which follows is at the discretion of both and to decide against furthering the acquaintance is not a breach of good manners. Bridge players are soon absorbed into the social life of any hotel and friendly, non-aggressive people find congenial company—if they want it—with reasonable ease wherever they stay.

Both short- and long-stay guests should appreciate that chairs and settees in the public rooms cannot be reserved by leaving newspapers, magazines or knitting upon them, except where the person is absent only for a few minutes.

Bedrooms and bathrooms should always be left tidy before going to breakfast so that chambermaids can get on with bed-making and the cleaning of rooms.

Morning tea and newspapers should be ordered the day of arrival. Shoes for cleaning should be put outside bedroom doors last thing at night. Keys should be left at the desk when guests go out and collected on their return.

Tipping

On the assumption that tipping is an etiquette problem and not a social question, gratuities should be given with a smile and a 'thank you' for personal service rendered. The only point then at issue is whom to tip, when to tip and how much to tip—and, of equal importance, whom not to tip.

Those in the latter group are: air hostesses and air stewards, pursers and ship's officers, a hotel proprietor and receptionist, a boarding house owner, the owner of a restaurant or business, the owner of a hair-dressing salon. Professional people are never tipped, and this includes nurses. Club servants receive a Christmas present but are not tipped. It is unnecessary to tip a petrol pump attendant regularly unless he gives extra service such as testing oil and water or wiping the windscreen of the car.

Hotels and restaurants
An increasing number of hotels and restaurants now have a service charge of 10% to 15% which is automatically added to the bill. Notice of this intent is usually printed on the brochure or tariff. In this case it is not obligatory to give more, but where staff, especially the chambermaid, table waiter and hall porter have given pleasantly efficient service, appreciation can be shown by means of a modest extra tip, thanking each individually. Where the service charge is not added, the 15% should be distributed between bedroom staff, dining room staff and hall staff before departure. Luggage porters, messenger boys and barmen who bring drinks to the table, are better tipped at the time of service, and the night porter if it is found necessary to knock him up in the small hours.

Cloakroom attendants in hotels, restaurants and shops are always tipped, the amount varying between 5p and 10p according to the establishment.

Boarding house servants are tipped.

Air journeys
Luggage porters who handle cases at the check-in desks on the outward journey and the luggage collection point on the return journey can be tipped but this is not obligatory.

Rail journeys
Luggage porters are tipped according to the number of cases and distance they are carried, the amount being usually 10p to 15p per case for a 'reasonable' journey, say from the train to the taxi rank. Dining car attendants receive a minimum of 10% of the bill.

Tipping at sea
Package cruises are usually inclusive of gratuities, otherwise the form is much the same as for hotels, around 15% of the fare being the accepted rate. This should be divided between the cabin steward or stewardess, bath steward, dining room steward and wine steward. Lounge and deck stewards are tipped at the time of service. In case of doubt, the Purser will be happy to advise.

Taxi journeys
Taxi drivers expect to receive around 5p for fares up to 25p, 10p for a 50p fare, and so on. There are no hard and fast rules but under-tipping is not recommended. After midnight larger tips are given.

Coach journeys

On long-distance coach tours, the driver and the courier should each receive a tip of 50p to 75p according to the distance covered and the duration of the tour. A collection is often made for the driver in command of day trips.

Sight-seeing trips
Semi-official and free-lance guides who show visitors round places of interest receive only modest remuneration and rely on tips to supplement their salaries. A tip of 15p per person is right and proper.

Hairdressers
In city salons at home and abroad a stylist would now expect a tip of 25p and the shampooist, 10p. Those giving extra attention (colour rinse, permanent wave, manicure) would expect a minimum of 10p. The coat attendant and coffee girl should be given a small tip too.

In private houses
When staying in a one-servant household, tip a cook-general or a working house-keeper £1 for a weekend stay. This can be handed to her in an envelope with a word of thanks. A lady house-keeper could be given flowers, chocolates, a scarf, a book token or similar gift—again with warm thanks. Where there is a cook and a housemaid, the cook should receive £1 and the housemaid 75p for a weekend stay.

Men invited for a weekend shoot should tip the gamekeeper and the loader, but as tips vary a good deal from house to house, it is advisable to ask a fellow guest or the host for guidance as to the acceptable amount. This also applies to grooms and hunt servants.

How to Obtain a Passport

British subjects wishing to travel abroad must obtain a passport. The application form should be completed and submitted with the fee, photographs and relevant documents at least three weeks before the passport is needed, and preferably longer. Applications submitted during the April to August period generally take longer to process than others.

There are two types of passport: a non-renewable British Visitor's Passport which is valid for one year, for short holiday visits to certain countries only; and a ten-year United Kingdom passport. British subjects may hold either passport, but not both. Present fees are given on page 155.

An application form for **a British Visitor's Passport** may be obtained from any main post office in England, Scotland and Wales, from local offices of the Department of Health and Social Services in Northern Ireland, and from the Passport Offices in Jersey, Guernsey and the Isle of Man.

When completed and signed, the form should be taken by the applicant, accompanied by his wife if she is to be included on the passport, to the issuing office, with a medical card or birth certificate or other acceptable form of identification (acceptable documents are listed on the form) for each person included in the application. The applicant must also supply two identical recent 'passport' photographs, plus, where necessary, two of his wife. Children under eight may not hold Visitor's passports; children over eight and under sixteen may either hold Visitor's passports in their own right, or be included on a parent's, older brother's, or older sister's; children aged sixteen and over must hold separate Visitor's passports. A Visitor's passport is not acceptable for use by the leader or deputy leader of a party of young people travelling on a collective passport.

A list of the countries for which a British Visitor's passport is valid during its year of issue is given on page 155.

An application form for **a United Kingdom Passport** may be obtained from main post offices in England, Scotland and Wales, from local offices of the Department of Health and Social Services in Northern Ireland, and from the regional Passport Offices listed on page 154.

Notes on how to complete the form are included. Once completed and signed, and counter-signed by a British subject who has known the applicant personally for at least two years and who is a minister of religion, police officer, doctor, or person of similar standing, the form should be taken or posted to the applicant's regional Passport Office (page 154), together with two identical 'passport'

photographs endorsed and signed by the person who signed the application, the fee (page 155), and the relevant documents (these are listed in the Notes for Guidance which are issued with the application form).

To obtain birth, adoption, or marriage certificates, follow the procedure described on page 151.

If you are getting married, and intend to travel abroad immediately after the wedding, you can obtain a special form for the issue of a separate post-dated United Kingdom passport in your future married name or for the amendment of your existing passport to show your future married name, or, if you wish to obtain a family passport for yourself and your future spouse, for the issue of a post-dated family passport. Visitor's passports, however, cannot be post-dated, nor issued in your future married name for use after marriage; no amendments can be made to them, once issued, nor can any extra applicants—no wives, no children—be added to them.

It may be that a situation could arise in which **you need to travel abroad urgently** but have no passport. In such cases, you should consult your regional Passport Office (page 154) at once, taking with you documentary evidence of the emergency. A duty officer is available to deal with cases of emergency which cannot be submitted during normal business hours (page 155). If you have already submitted an application, and an emergency arises before the passport has been issued, so that you need it with all possible haste, consult the office concerned. You will need to give your name, the place and date of your birth, the date on which the application was lodged, whether it was sent by post or handed in personally, and if the latter, the date and the reference number on your receipt.

If you lose your passport abroad, notify the nearest British Consul at once; if at home, tell the police and the issuing office immediately.

Manners and Customs
on the Continent

People are what they are wherever they are, and those who observe normal courtesies at home will do so abroad, adapting themselves unobtrusively to their surroundings and quietly observing and conforming to the customs of each country they visit. Most people are anxious not to offend, although there are ill-bred travellers everywhere: fortunately they are still in a minority and have not yet discoloured the image of the majority who give a good account of themselves and leave an impression of a well-mannered, well-informed island people.

Customs vary widely and Europe alone poses many problems with its diverse cultures. Only by careful study or close contact over a lengthy period can anyone hope to master the intricacies and nuances of its social language, but the following may help towards an understanding of the civilities of daily life.

In France it is customary to shake hands with people at every meeting and open every conversation with *'Bonjour, Madame'* or *Bonjour, Monsieur'*. A Frenchman will always remove his hat when entering a lift and stand aside to let a woman leave first; respond, *'Merci, Monsieur'*. It is considered a breach of good manners to wear sports clothes or sun-bathing dress in restaurants and hotels. The utmost propriety should be observed in churches and all places of worship, conversation being conducted in quiet tones, dress being modest and strictly cover-up. The rule that women must wear a hat or a head-scarf when entering a Roman Catholic church has been greatly relaxed, but it is still courteous to do so. Curb drill is strictly observed and it is unwise and ill-mannered to defy police on point duty. A French hostess is always sent flowers, but never chrysanthemums, which are considered 'the flowers of the Dead' and placed in French cemeteries on All Souls Day. It is customary to tip the wine waiter in an hotel or restaurant, and the usherette who shows patrons to their seats in theatre or cinema is usually given a modest 50 centimes per person. Address the waiter as *'Monsieur'*, never as *'Garçon'*.

In Belgium and Holland it is customary to send flowers to the hostess after a meal in a private house. In Belgium theatre and cinema usherettes are always tipped, in Holland they usually are. In some homes it is customary to smoke between courses, this on the premise that it is impolite to rush through a meal which has taken the hostess some time to prepare.

In Switzerland a tea-time guest takes flowers to her hostess, presenting these unwrapped. Visitors should note that it is an offence to scatter litter in the streets, and in many places an offence to appear in public places and on river steamers shirtless or in abbreviated dress. Restaurants and hotels automatically add a service charge to their bills and extra tips are given only for exceptional service. Cinema and theatre usherettes expect a small tip.

In Spain the authorities frown on bikinis, and deplore the wearing of sunbathing dress away from the beaches. Head-scarves or hats and cover-up dress are essential when in church, and men are expected to take off their hats when funerals or religious processions go by. Visitors should beware of becoming involved in political arguments or making adverse comments on the state of the country. There is no compulsion to attend bullfights and it is better to stay away than arouse antagonism by offensive remarks and behaviour. Theatre and cinema usherettes are usually tipped 1 or 2 pesetas and the shoe-shine boys should be given a small tip if used.

In Italy women visiting churches should cover their arms, wear a skirt which isn't too mini, and, as a courtesy, can also cover the head. Theatre and cinema usherettes are tipped between 50 and 100 lire.

In Scandinavian countries punctuality is of the greatest importance when being entertained privately. A service charge is almost always added to hotel and restaurant bills and only very small extra tips are offered.

In Germany and Austria it is essential to sit down to meals correctly dressed and men should not appear in shirt sleeves and without ties. Most Germans speak English and understand very well the anti-Nazi feeling still lingering abroad without visitors going out of their way to re-live the two wars. Guests should check whether a service charge has been added to hotel and restaurant bills—it may not have been.

In Yugoslavia it is best to avoid political discussion. The service charge is not normally added to hotel and restaurant bills; 10% is the expected rate.

In Greece a minimum tip of 10% must be added to the restaurant bill and a small additional tip should be given to the junior waiter who helps the table waiter as he does not share in the staff *tronc*. Theatre and cinema usherettes are tipped and the shoe-shine boys if used. It is wise and courteous to obey notices about swimming and sunbathing gear. Women should never look or go behind the screen in churches, men only if invited; and it is polite to purchase and light a candle—though the attendant will probably pinch this out economically as you turn away.

In Malta it is still customary for women to cover their heads and arms on entering churches, and beach notices request and require fairly decorous dress.

In the U.S.S.R. tipping is not accepted practice as yet, and no tip would be expected at hotels, restaurants, hairdressers, etc. Taxi-drivers may be offered a small tip but would not expect this automatically. A modest souvenir of Britain would be more welcome in most cases.

The Engagement

Becoming engaged

Whilst it is no longer considered necessary for a young man to obtain the permission of a girl's father before proposing to her, it is still an act of courtesy to see her parents before making public the engagement, and to tell his own family the good news. It is then for the girl's mother to announce the engagement in local or national newspapers on the following lines:

> *Mr T. M. Brown*
> *   Miss F. R. Jones*
> *The engagement is announced between Timothy, son of Mr and Mrs E. P.*
> *Brown of Haywards Heath, Sussex, and Fiona Rosalind, eldest daughter*
> *of Major and Mrs T. Jones of Amersham, Bucks*

or, if the date of the wedding has been fixed:

> *Mr C. Dark*
> *   Miss P. I. Light*
> *A marriage has been arranged and will take place shortly between Charles,*
> *son of Mr and Mrs B. Dark of Reading, Berkshire, and Patricia Imogen,*
> *youngest daughter of Mr and Mrs D. R. Light of Altrincham, Cheshire.*

When the engagement becomes official, the young man usually seals the pact with a ring, which his fiancée is privileged to choose—with a sympathetic eye to his means, of course. There are many beautiful stones apart from diamonds, and lovely antique rings can be found.

The engagement period should be a happy time of socialising and planning for the wedding and the young couple will want to spend as much time as possible together. The young man should receive the 'congratulations' of friends, his fiancée receives their 'good wishes' and 'felicitations'. Invitations should be extended to both—not to either one separately at this time. All the world loves a lover, but too much kissing and embracing in public places is an embarrassment to the British, although a kiss of greeting and farewell is not only right and proper, but should be encouraged.

Breaking an engagement

No matter what the circumstances are which lead to the breaking of an engagement it should always be done kindly and with dignity, sparing hurt as much as possible and without public recrimination. If an announcement is made, it should be brief:

The marriage arranged between Mr T. Thomas and Miss G. Davies will not now take place.

The engagement ring must be returned, and it is usual to return or to destroy any letters. Wedding presents must also be sent back with a brief note.

A girl may like to confide in near friends, but on the whole it is better to remain quite silent and so close an unfortunate chapter.

A letter breaking an engagement is supremely personal, and only the most general guidelines can be given. Write simply and directly, sparing the fiancé's feelings. Perhaps something like this:

My dear John,

When we became engaged last November we were two very happy people and I never thought anything could happen which might interfere with our plans for an early marriage or mar the joy we found in each other. Since then nothing drastic has happened in our lives, yet we have gradually changed towards one another in attitude as well as thought and I am now so disenchanted that I can no longer face the prospect of a life together. I hope you will understand and forgive me if this causes you pain, but I am sure that a broken engagement is better than a marriage failure. Please believe, John, that I wish you well for the future.

Yours ———

The Marriage

The law

A couple wishing to marry in the United Kingdom must be aged sixteen or over; in England, Wales and Northern Ireland, anyone aged between sixteen and eighteen who wishes to marry must have parental consent, as described in the section on the Marriage of Minors, below, but this is not a legal requirement in Scotland. They must both be free to marry, and sane; they must not be related, either by blood or by marriage, within the forbidden degrees, though it is legally permissible to marry a former partner's sister, aunt or niece (brother, uncle or nephew) or the former partner of your own brother, uncle or nephew (sister, aunt or niece); it should be noted that in Northern Ireland marriage with a former partner's sister, aunt, etc., is only permitted if the former partner has died. Residential qualifications must normally be fulfilled, though these are not required in the case of marriage by Special Licence; the various formalities are described in greater detail later in this chapter.

These formalities apart, a couple wishing to marry according to the rites of a particular faith or sect may have to fulfil other formalities; examples of these are given in the section on Ceremonies which begins on page 108.

Any foreigner who proposes to marry within the United Kingdom, whether to a British subject or to someone of his own nationality and creed, should first consult his resident representative in Britain to ascertain whether such a marriage is acceptable and binding at law both here and in his own country. A similar check should be made by a British subject marrying a foreigner.

The marriage of minors

The law requires that in England, Wales and Northern Ireland, anyone aged between sixteen and eighteen who wishes to marry must have the written permission of his or her parents or legal guardians. If both parents are alive, their joint signatures should appear on the letter or document of consent. If one or both parents are resident abroad, the signature(s) should be witnessed by a responsible person, such as a notary or a consul. If there is any difficulty about obtaining the consent of the parents or legal guardians, consult the local superintendent registrar (his address is in the telephone directory) and he will be able to advise you in the matter. In Northern Ireland consent must be given on a special form and witnessed by specified witnesses.

Where a minor feels that permission is unreasonably withheld, he or she can approach the Courts for the necessary consent to marry.

Formalities preceding marriage according to the rites of the Church of England

There are four ways of marrying according to the rites of the Church of England: by Banns, by Common Licence, by Special Licence and by Certificate issued by the Superintendent Registrar of Marriages—the last seldom used.

Marriage by banns: *'I publish the banns of marriage between John James Reid, bachelor, of the parish of St Peter, Barchester, and Philippa Mary Wright, spinster, of this parish. This is for the first time of asking. If any of you know cause or just impediment why these persons may not be joined together in Holy Matrimony, you are to declare it.'* Seven days' notice must be given to the incumbent before the calling of banns. Only one of the parties need make the application and when the clergyman has satisfied himself that both parties are free to marry, and has signified his willingness to perform the ceremony, he will arrange for audible publication of the banns on three separate Sundays. Should the bride and groom live in different parishes, banns must be published in each; the wedding may take place in either parish—the final word on this being the bride's prerogative. If the bride or groom regularly worships in a church which is not the parish church of either party, and if they wish to marry there and the incumbent is willing, then they may do so, providing they are on the Electoral Roll of that church and that banns are published in the respective parish churches and in the church where the ceremony will take place.

After the publication of banns, and as long as no objection has been raised, the ceremony may take place on any date within the three-month-period of validity, by arrangement with the clergyman.

By special Act of Parliament a chaplain or commanding officer can publish for three successive Sundays **on board ship, the banns** of men and women serving in the Royal Navy. This, together with the Certificate of Publication he will then issue, and the calling of banns in the parish of the second party to the marriage, will enable the ceremony to take place in that church in the ordinary way without a Special Licence.

Marriage by Common Licence: personal or written application for the licence must be made either to the clergyman who is the local Surrogate of Marriages, or to the local Bishop's Diocesan Registry, or to the Master of Faculties at the Faculty Office in London (the address is given on page 155). A sworn affidavit will be required stating that there is no legal impediment to the marriage and that the church proposed for the wedding is situated in the parish where either the bride or the groom has resided for at least fifteen days prior to the application, or is the usual place of worship of the bride or the groom. The Licence is valid on the day of issue and remains in force for three months, after which date a fresh application must be made.

Marriage by Special Licence: a Special Licence is granted only in exceptional circumstances and where conditions are such that an ordinary Common Licence would not suffice. It enables a marriage to be solemnised according to Church of England rites at any time and in any place in England and Wales, and it is only issued on the authority of the Archbishop of Canterbury, through the Faculty Office in London.

Marriage by Certificate issued by a Superintendent Registrar: it is unusual for marriage according to Church of England rites to be celebrated on the authority of a Registrar's Certificate; the marriage can be solemnized in church only if the clergymen agrees to it, and he is not obliged to do so and can, if he wishes, insist on a Common Licence—thus he should be consulted before any plans are made. The procedure for obtaining the Certificate is as described below: application should be made at least twenty-one days prior to the intended marriage, and the bride and groom should have been resident in the District for not less than seven days before the notice is entered. The Certificate is valid for three months.

Formalities preceding civil marriage and marriage according to the rites of other religions, in England and Wales

A civil marriage, and marriages according to the rites of other faiths, such as the Free Churches, the Roman Catholic Church, or the Society of Friends, take place on the authority of a certificate(s) with or without a licence, issued by a superintendent registrar.

Civil marriages, which are often called 'Register Office' marriages, take place in a register office and are performed by a superintendent registrar in the presence of a registrar of marriages and of two witnesses. The ceremony is described on page 108.

Marriage according to the rites of the Free Churches and of the Roman Catholic Church can take place, once the certificate has been issued, only in the building registered for the solemnization of marriages named in the certificate(s). If an 'authorised person' is present to register the marriage, there is no need for the registrar to attend, but failing this he must be asked to do so; the bride and groom must check with their minister and with the superintendent registrar whether this will be necessary. The marriage must take place between eight in the morning and six at night, with open doors, in the presence of at least two witnesses, and the ceremony must include one of the accepted forms of the legal declaration. More details about actual ceremonies are given on pages 111 to 113.

Marriage according to the usage of the Society of Friends is subject to the approval of their Registering Officers. It can take place, once the certificate(s) has been issued, in a Friends' Meeting House or other place regularly used for Quaker worship, and must be registered by the Registering Officer appointed by the Society; the registrar does not attend.

Marriage according to Jewish rites may take place once the certificate(s) has been issued, only in the synagogue or other place named in the certificate(s), and must be registered by the secretary of the synagogue of which the groom is a member; the registrar does not attend.

Marriage according to Church of England rites may also take place on the authority of a superintendent registrar's certificate, though this is unusual; it is described in more detail on page 97.

Formalities preceding marriage in England and Wales, on the authority of a certificate issued by a superintendent registrar, with or without a licence
A certificate is issued by a superintendent registrar. Notice of marriage must be given personally to the superintendent registrar in the district where the couple have resided for a minimum period of seven days. If the bride and groom reside in different districts, separate notices must be given in both, and the same residential requirements apply; the certificates of both superintendent registrars must be obtained before the marriage can take place. The marriage must normally take place in the district in which one of the parties resides. The address of the superintendent registrar can be found in the telephone book, under *Registration of Births, Deaths and Marriages,* and it is wise to telephone in advance to check office hours.

If one party lives in England or Wales and the other in Scotland, the one living in England or Wales should apply for a certificate in the usual way, and the one resident in Scotland should give notice to his district registrar as described in the next section, or apply to the receiver of banns, session clerk or minister to have banns proclaimed (if banns are called, the certificate of proclamation of banns, described in the next section, must be issued *before* notice can be given to a superintendent registrar in England or Wales).

If one party lives in England or Wales and the other in Northern Ireland, the one living in England or Wales should give notice to the superintendent registrar and obtain a certificate as described above. The party living in Northern Ireland should serve notice and obtain a certificate from his registrar (he or she must reside in the district for seven days preceding the service of notice, and twenty-one clear days must pass after the date of entry of notice before the registrar may issue his certificate). A Northern Ireland registrar of marriages may grant a certificate for a marriage to be solemnized in England or

Wales (although he cannot grant a licence for such a marriage); but if the couple propose to marry in an Anglican church in England or Wales, they must first obtain the incumbent's consent to act on a certificate issued in Northern Ireland.

When you give notice to the superintendent registrar to obtain a certificate, you will be asked to give details of name, age, marital status, address, duration of residence and occupation. You will be required to make a declaration that there is no legal obstacle to the marriage, and show proof of widowhood or divorce if you have been married before. If you are over sixteen but under eighteen, you must have obtained parental consent, as described on page 95.

The superintendent registrar's certificate authorising the marriage is issued twenty-one clear days after the notice is entered, and is valid for three months from the date of entry. During the twenty-one days, notice of the couple's intent of marrying is posted and on view to the public.

Fees at the time of publication are given on page 156.

A licence is issued on personal application by one of the parties to the superintendent registrar of the district in which the marriage is to take place, providing he or she has lived in the district for a period of fifteen days prior to notice being given; the other party can reside anywhere in England or Wales, but not elsewhere in the United Kingdom or abroad. The same details will be required as for the superintendent registrar's certificate alone. Fees are quoted on page 156. Notice of intent to marry is not posted, and if no objection to the marriage is raised, the licence can be issued two or three days after the entry of notice. If a religious ceremony is to be held, such arrangements should only be made after consulting the minister.

The issue of a Registrar-General's licence enables non-Anglicans to marry at any time in unregistered premises when one of them is seriously ill and unlikely to recover.

Formalities preceding marriage in Scotland

The basic conditions for a marriage in Scotland have been described on page 95. The marriage may be solemnized, after due notice as described below, by a minister, clergyman, pastor or priest of any Christian denomination, or by a registrar of births, deaths and marriages authorised by the Registrar General to conduct civil marriages. Providing the conditions given below have been fulfilled, and that there are two witnesses present, religious marriages may be solemnised in any place and at any time; civil marriages must take place, again in the presence of two witnesses, in the registration office of an authorised registrar.

All marriages in Scotland must be preceded by Proclamation of Banns, or Publication of Notice, or Sheriff's Licence. A note about fees is given on page

156. A certificate of proclamation of banns is not acceptable for a civil marriage; and a minister of the Church of Scotland is not bound to perform a marriage unless banns have been proclaimed, although he may do so if he wishes.

Proclamation of Banns: both parties must have resided in the registration district for fifteen clear days immediately preceding the application for proclamation (the day of arrival in the district does not count). If bride and groom live in different districts, banns must be proclaimed in both, or one must proceed by banns and the other by Publication of Notice (below). The application must be made to the receiver of banns, session clerk or minister of a Church of Scotland church which has been appointed by the Presbytery of the district as a church in which banns may be proclaimed. He will arrange for the banns to be proclaimed during the principal service on one or two successive Sundays (strict law and tradition differ on this point). A certificate of proclamation of banns will then be issued, and this should be taken to the registrar of births, deaths and marriages for the district in which the marriage is to take place. It is valid for three months.

Publication of Notice: application can only be made to the registrar for the district in which the applicant (or applicants if they live in the same one) has his usual residence or has resided for a period of fifteen clear days before application. The applicant must sign the Notice before two householders who must declare that they believe the facts given by him to be true. The registrar will then display a Notice of Marriage on his notice board, and after display for seven clear days (the day on which the notice is first displayed does not count), a Certificate of Publication of Notice, valid for three months, will be issuable, provided that no objections have been lodged and the registrar has no grounds for believing that there is any impediment to the marriage.

Sheriff's Licence: this is granted at the discretion of the sheriff and only if there is a reasonable excuse for the parties not having banns proclaimed or notice published in the usual way. Either the bride or the groom must have his or her usual residence in Scotland, or have resided there for the fifteen days immediately preceding application. They must make a joint application to the sheriff within whose jurisdiction the marriage is to take place and the services of a solicitor are usually necessary. A sheriff's licence is valid for ten days.

A couple wishing to have a church wedding should obtain their certificate, or licence, as described, and take it to the registrar for the district in which the marriage is to take place. The registrar will complete and give to the parties a **Marriage Schedule,** containing particulars which they supply to him, and this must be shown to the minister who is to solemnise the marriage. Immediately after the religious ceremony it must be signed by the minister, the bride, the groom, and two witnesses. It must be returned to the issuing registrar within

100

three days to enable him to register the marriage.

A couple wishing to have a register office wedding should call at the registrar's office, arrange for the publication of notice (or obtain a sheriff's licence), and provide information for the marriage schedule.

Across-the-border marriages

There are special arrangements for Scots who wish to marry in England, or who wish to contract a marriage in Scotland though they or their partner is or are resident in England; and also for Scots marrying foreigners abroad. Registrars of births, deaths and marriages should be consulted about these. Similarly Scots wishing to marry in Wales or Northern Ireland, or wishing to marry in Scotland though they or their partner is or are resident elsewhere in the United Kingdom, should ask the advice of their district registrar.

Formalities preceding marriage in Northern Ireland

The minimum age for marriage in Northern Ireland is sixteen. If either party is over sixteen but under eighteen, the written consent of parents or guardians, or a Court order dispensing with the need for such consent, must first be obtained and submitted, properly witnessed, on the specified form.

Church of Ireland

If the bride or groom or both are Protestant Episcopalians, marriage may take place by licence, special licence (granted by a bishop), or registrar's certificate (page 103). If both are Protestant Episcopalians, it can take place by banns.

Banns are published in much the same way as banns in the Church of England but the marriage must take place in the parish church of one party.

A licence is obtainable from the Church of Ireland licenser for marriages in churches within his district. To obtain it, either the bride or the groom must have resided in the district for at least seven days immediately before service of the notice, and this must be given at least seven days before the issue of the licence. The licenser must send copies of the notice to the clergymen of the places of worship which the bride and groom attend. Before the licence is issued, one of the parties must make an oath or declaration including a statement that for at least fourteen days immediately before the day of grant of the licence, one of them has been living in the district attached to the church where the marriage is to take place. The marriage must take place within three months of the date of notice.

Presbyterians

If the bride or the groom or both are Presbyterians, their marriage may take place by licence or by special licence. If they are both Presbyterians, it can take place by banns.

Banns are published in the church or churches of which the bride and groom are members. The minister needs six days' notice. The banns must be published on three Sundays preceding the marriage, and the marriage must take place in the church, or in one of the two churches, in which this is done.

A licence is obtainable from a licensing minister. He is appointed by a presbytery and deals with applications for marriage licences in churches within that presbytery. At least seven days before the issue of a licence, the bride or groom must give the licensing minister a certificate from the minister of the congregation to which he or she has belonged for at least a month; this certificate is to the effect that notice has been given. Immediately before the licence is granted, he or she must also make an oath or declaration which includes a statement that one or other party to the marriage has been living within the presbytery, in his or her usual place of residence, for the fifteen days immediately before. The marriage must take place within three months of the date of entry of notice in the licensing minister's book, and within one calendar month of the date of the licence.

A special licence may be granted by the Moderator of the Presbyterian body. It authorises marriage at any time and in any place in Northern Ireland.

Roman Catholic Church

If both parties are Roman Catholic, they should apply to their parish priest or priests for **information** about the steps preceding their marriage. If only one party is a Roman Catholic, the couple may marry in a Roman Catholic church on the authority of **a licence** issued by a licenser appointed by a bishop (notice must be given seven days before the issue of a licence, and the licenser must send copies of the notice to the clergymen of the couple's places of worship), or on the authority of **a registrar's certificate,** obtained as described below.

Registrar's office marriages, and marriages according to the usages of other denominations

Marriages in registrars' offices and marriages according to usages of other religious bodies may take place by a licence issued by a district registrar of marriages, by registrar's certificate, or, if one or both parties belong to the Baptist Church, the Congregational Union of Ireland, or the Methodist or Wesleyan Church in Ireland, by special licence.

A registrar may issue **a licence** authorising a marriage in a church or registered building in his District, or in his office. If both parties live in the same District, one must reside there for not less than fifteen days and the other for not less than seven days immediately preceding the service of notice. Copies of the notice will be sent to the ministers of the places of worship usually attended by the parties and to the minister of the place of worship where the marriage is to take place; or, if the marriage is to take place in the registrar's office and either party has not attended a customary place of worship during the month preceding notice, notice will be published in a newspaper. Seven clear days after the entry of notice the registrar may, after administering an oath or declaration to one of the parties, on the lines described above, issue the licence. If the parties reside in different districts, notice must be given in both, and each party must fulfil a fifteen-day residential qualification. The registrar of the district in which the marriage is to take place will require the certificate of the registrar of the other district before he issues a licence.

A registrar may issue **a certificate,** without a licence, authorising a marriage in a church or registered building in his District, or in his office. The procedure followed is similar to that described in the last paragraph, excepting that the period of residence immediately preceding the service of notice is not less than seven days, and the registrar may not issue a certificate until twenty-one clear days from the date of entry of notice.

The marriage must take place within three months of the date of notice.

Marriage according to **Jewish rites** can take place in Northern Ireland only by registrar's certificate.

Marriage according to the usages of the **Society of Friends** is subject to the approval of their registering officers. It can be solemnised by registrar's certificate in a Friends' meeting-house, or by special licence at any time and in any place.

Arrangements and attendants

The success of every social function is dependent upon constructive planning and co-ordination and none more so than a wedding. Three questions must be resolved before any arrangements can be put into operation: where, when and how will the wedding take place?

The first decision is by tradition the prerogative of the bride. Does she want a civil ceremony or a church wedding? And if the latter, does she wish to marry, as is traditional, in her own parish church?

The form of the marriage can only be settled after discussion between the young couple and, assuming that the traditional arrangement about expenses is being followed (page 125), the bride's parents, whose financial resources are, or should be, the determining factor. A fully choral service with choir, organ and pealing bells is an expensive undertaking, and needs careful thought.

So too does the guest list. If the bride's parents are paying for the reception, then the final word on this rests with them and the couple should trim numbers accordingly. It is also wise to check how many guests the church or Register office will hold.

The bridal pair should then make an appointment to see the minister concerned, to discuss dates and times for the wedding. If, out of personal friendship or for family or sentimental reasons, they would like to invite some other minister who is an ordained priest of the Church of England to conduct the ceremony, they must ask the incumbent if he will agree to this (page 44). The choice of music, psalms and hymns is also subject to the minister's approval. Some traditional wedding hymns are *The King of love my shepherd is, Love Divine all loves excelling* and *O Perfect Love. The Voice that breath'd o'er Eden* is an old favourite. *All creatures of our God and King, All people that on earth do dwell* (The Old Hundredth), *Immortal invisible God only wise,* and *Praise my soul the King of heaven* are well-known hymns of praise and joy; *Father hear the prayer we offer* strikes a different, more sober note. *God is love, his the care* is jubilant and perhaps a little more unusual; *O Brother Man, fold to thy heart thy brother* is a quieter choice.

Only when these arrangements are completed can the bride's mother order the invitations and the service leaflets; and before doing so, she will also need to know where the reception is to be held. Will it be at home, at a hall or an hotel? Who is to undertake the catering, make the wedding cake and provide the wine? Many catering firms have banqueting rooms which can be hired and will, like hotels, provide everything necessary, including changing rooms for the use of bride and groom before they leave for the honeymoon. Look in the Yellow Pages section of the local telephone directory, or in the local paper or parish magazine. Estimates can be obtained and compared.

An example of the wording for a wedding invitation appears on page 46. If guests are being invited to the reception only, follow the style of wording shown on page 48. The invitations should be issued three to six weeks prior to the ceremony, as until the replies have been received the bride's mother won't know how many to cater for—though it is usual for about two-thirds to accept. The bridegroom's parents, the best man and the bridesmaids need not receive invitation cards, since it is taken for granted that they will attend, but it is usual for the bride's mother to send each an invitation with a note saying that she is sure they would like a memento of the ceremony.

Local printers are usually happy to advise on the lay-out and wording of the service leaflets. It is not essential to provide these, since the church usually has an ample supply of prayer books and hymn books (though if the wedding is a large one, it is sensible to check this too), but they are a pleasant memento.

The bridesmaids are chosen by the bride from her immediate family and friends, though it is usual for her to ask someone from the groom's family as well. They should look decorative and enhance the occasion. Generally speaking, the bride chooses their dresses but adult bridesmaids pay for their own and smaller ones are equipped by their mothers. The section called *Wardrobe for Hire,* on page 78, may be of help here.

The attendants' duties are not onerous. The bridesmaids gather at the bride's home and are driven to the church in the car preceding hers, to arrive a few minutes in advance. They await the bride in the church porch and then follow her up the aisle in formation, standing behind her during the service. When arranging who is to walk with whom in this procession, remember that **the chief bridesmaid** should be on the left-hand side, usually pairing with the second bridesmaid, so that she can step forward behind the bride and take her bouquet or gloves before the service begins, thus leaving the bride's hands free for the ceremony of putting on the ring. (If the bride wishes to bestow a ring on the groom, this may be in the chief bridesmaid's charge, and handed over at the appropriate point.) She returns the bouquet to the bride at the end of the service before the procession to the vestry for the signing of the register, and accompanies her into the vestry where she helps her to throw back her veil before signing her maiden name—for the last time. For the recessional, the bridesmaids follow behind the bridal pair in exactly the same order as for the procession up the aisle.

Small bridesmaids and pages should be young enough to lend enchantment, but old enough to get through the service without causing distraction. Some brides like to pair pages and small bridesmaids in the procession, but to have a single adult bridesmaid, who will usually proceed unpartnered up the aisle, step forward to take the bouquet, attend the bride into the vestry, and may, if liked, be partnered by a close male relative, such as the bride's brother, for the recessional down the aisle.

The best man is usually a brother, close friend or relative of the bridegroom. Traditionally he is a bachelor, though this is no longer strictly observed. He should be calm, dependable, tactful and business-like. He accompanies the groom to church and either before or after the ceremony attends to all disbursements on his behalf: clergy and church fees, payments to the organist, choir, bell-ringer and verger. The wedding ring is in his charge and he must produce this at the appropriate moment. He waits with the bridegroom in the front right-hand pew until the bride arrives, sitting on the groom's right; steps forward with him; and stands behind him and slightly to his right during the service. He accompanies the bridal party to the vestry for the signing of the register and often acts as chief witness, but he does not generally take part in the recessional, his duty being to make his way with all possible speed to the church door to organise the photographers and see that the bridal car is in readiness and other cars in line to proceed to the reception in correct order.

The ushers are the bride's brothers and any other personable young men of both families. They should be at the church in good time. Their duty is to greet the guests on arrival at the church and ask 'Bride or groom?', ushering relations and friends of the bride into pews on the left-hand side, and those of the bridegroom into pews on the right, and seeing that the immediate family have seats in the front three pews. They often also help to distribute button-holes and service-sheets and where necessary, to direct the cars.

In addition to choosing attendants and ushers, the bride may need to invite a **friend to escort her** up the aisle and to 'give her away'. Traditionally, of course, this role is her father's, but if he has died it is usual for her to ask some other relative or a family friend. If her parents are separated or divorced, she may wish to ask her father to take his traditional part or, if her relationship with her step-father has been a long and happy one, she may invite him to stand for her; if however she wishes to avoid making a direct choice between the two, she may ask a grandfather or a godfather or a brother to escort her: quiet tact and a concern for the bride's happiness on 'her' day can do much to ease the situation. Although traditionally the role is taken by a man, some brides have been given away by a widowed mother, godmother or sister.

The attendants have been chosen, their outfits purchased or hired; the bride has chosen or hired her own dress, with gloves and hat or head-dress; the groom and the best man and ushers have arranged to hire morning dress, if this is to be worn, as has the bride's escort. The bridegroom has bought the ring. It is advisable to book a hair appointment in good time; and the bride and her bridesmaids may like to show the stylist the head-dress to be worn so that a suitable hair-style can be devised.

The organist and the choir should also have been booked, and the ringers if the bells are to be rung. Bells should be pealed for twenty minutes before the arrival of the bride, and for the same length of time when the ceremony is over, thus allowing for the main party to leave the church and get away to the reception while they are still ringing.

Cars must be booked as well: usually the bridegroom arranges for one to take him and his best man to the church, and the bride's father books three—more if grandparents or other relatives have to be driven to the church; the first is for his wife, usually with a male relative to accompany her, the second for the bridesmaids and pages, and the third for himself and the bride. The car hire firm will decorate the cars with white bridal ribbons. The groom should also book a car to take him and his wife from the reception to the station or airport.

The photographer should be booked in advance. Some brides want to have the wedding filmed or tape-recorded; check this with the minister first, and ask him at the same time if photos may be taken inside the church and during the ceremony. It is also as well to check whether he allows the throwing of confetti: many ministers, faced with a drift of pink paper to clear up, Saturday after Saturday, have now asked wedding parties to refrain from confetti-throwing, and their wishes should be respected. A minister may, however, be willing for guests to shower the bride with flower petals or rice, and if so, the ushers should have supplies to hand and tactfully check anyone who has brought the paper variety.

The flowers must also be ordered. With the bridal gown and the bridesmaids' dresses chosen, the florist should be consulted on seasonal flowers which will complement both. Posies are always popular, and flower-balls are coming into fashion. Some brides like to carry a prayer book with a spray of flowers attached. Others may wish for fresh flower head-dresses. Also to be ordered are flowers for the reception hall and tables, button-holes for the men-folk—single carnations without greenery—and sprays or corsages for the bride's mother, the groom's mother, and the grandmothers. It is usual to decorate the church with flowers and it is sensible to arrange in advance who is to do this and at what time, and to ask whether any other weddings are taking place in the church on the same day and if so, to get in touch with the parties concerned and arrange for flowers in keeping with both colour schemes.

In the case of a large important wedding, it is almost essential to hold a rehearsal; it is not necessary for the bride and her attendants to wear their bridal clothes, but if the bride intends to wear a train or a veil which the child attendants are to carry, they must be shown how to do this with a mock train fixed to her day dress or with a makeshift veil. A suitable time for the rehearsal must, of course, be arranged with the minister and the verger.

The bride's mother has one more essential duty—not an easy assignment. This is to keep her daughter from succumbing to pre-wedding nerves by seeing that she is not fretted by unnecessary anxieties and that she gets plenty of sleep.

Ceremonies

The civil ceremony

A Register Office wedding is short and simple, and the arrangements described in the last section may be modified accordingly. When giving notice of marriage—or, if they wish, before doing so—the couple may like to ask the superintendent registrar how many guests he can accommodate; many register offices can take quite large parties. If the guest list is kept short, it is not essential to have formal invitation cards; hand-written notes can be sent instead. If, however, formal invitations are issued, the general principles outlined on page 46 may be followed. Arrangements should be made for the reception—some couples like to have a family lunch or a formal reception in a hotel or restaurant, others prefer to give a large informal party later on when they return from their honeymoon. Many 'white weddings' now take place in register offices, and are in fact becoming more popular; alternatively the bride chooses a pretty dress—perhaps a long one in Laura Ashley style—and may like to wear a hat or a scrap of veiling. She may ask a sister or close friend to act as her bridesmaid if she wishes to keep the ceremony simple, or may invite a number of bridesmaids to attend her if she prefers. The bridegroom may like to ask a friend to act as best man or chief witness. Cars and photographers should be booked in advance where necessary, but the taking of photographs during the ceremony is not allowed. It is usual for the bride and bridesmaid to carry sprays of flowers, for the bridegroom and his witness to wear button-holes, for the mothers to be given corsages. Some registrars supply flowers to decorate the office and the waiting room.

In general, the ceremony is a very simple one, the bridegroom and the bride making the customary declarations in front of the superintendent registrar, the two witnesses, and the other guests—'I do solemnly declare that I know not of any lawful impediment why I, Peter Edward Bush, may not be joined in matrimony to Clare Elizabeth Greer'—and then the customary promises—'I call upon these persons here present to witness that I, Clare Elizabeth Greer, do take thee, Peter Edward Bush, to be my lawful wedded husband.' Provision is made for the giving and exchange of rings in the course of the ceremony.

An Anglican Service of Blessing

It is possible to have a service of blessing held in an Anglican church following a civil marriage, and those who feel they would derive spiritual comfort from this—including the divorced—should consult their parish priest. The service is discretionary, the decision resting with the bishop of the diocese, although in some areas consent has been given for the priest to act on his own initiative.

108

The Church of England ceremony

The traditional church wedding has always an air of fairytale splendour which is accentuated as the bells peal out in gladness to welcome the ethereal bride, with her bridesmaids and pages assembled in readiness in the church porch. The guests have been greeted by the ushers, given Order of Service leaflets or prayer books and hymnals, and shown to their places—friends and relations of the groom on the right of the nave, those of the bride on the left, close relatives in the second and third pews from the front. The bridegroom and his best man have taken their places in the front right-hand pew. The bride's mother has been escorted by a son or male member of the family to the front left-hand pew, leaving the outer seat vacant for her husband to step into when he has given away the bride. The organ plays softly, and all wait for the change of tempo which signifies that the great moment has arrived.

The bells fall silent. The bridegroom and his best man move from their pew to their place at the chancel steps, the best man standing to the right of the groom and a little behind him. The bride on her father's right arm (page 106) is led slowly forward up the aisle, her attendants in procession behind her. The officiating clergy may await her at the chancel steps, or may move slowly down the nave towards the procession and then turn to precede it, the bridegroom turning to smile a greeting as his bride is led to his left side. So they stand in readiness for the service: from left to right, the bride's father, the bride, the bridegroom and the best man. The chief bridesmaid steps unobtrusively forward and relieves the bride of her bouquet, gloves or prayer book, while behind them, completing the picture, bridesmaids and pages stand in pairs.

The marriage service now begins with an address from the clergyman. For the last time he asks whether there is any cause or just impediment to the marriage—'As ye will answer at the dreadful day of judgment'—and then puts the formal question to the bridegroom:

'Wilt thou have this Woman to thy wedded wife, to live together after God's ordinance in the holy estate of Matrimony? Wilt thou love her, comfort her, honour and keep her in sickness and in health, and, forsaking all others, keep thee only unto her, so long as ye both shall live?'

The man shall answer: 'I will.'

The clergyman then questions the bride. In the old service she was, and is, asked if she will 'obey' her husband, 'serve him, love, honour, and keep him'; under the 'new' service, however, which she is free to choose, she does not promise to obey.

The clergyman then asks: 'Who giveth this Woman to be married to this Man?' It is traditional for the bride's father or 'friend' (page 106) to reply 'I do', though no mention of this is made in the Book of Common Prayer, his duty

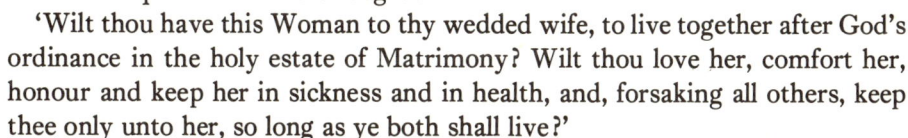

109

being simply to pass his daughter's right hand to the clergyman, palm downwards. The clergyman joins the couple's right hands, and the bride's father steps back and joins his wife in the front left-hand pew.

The couple then plight their troth, the bridegroom repeating the words after the clergyman as he takes the bride's right hand in his own, and then freeing her hand, so that she in her turn may take his right hand in her own and repeat the promise:

'I, Philippa Mary, take thee, John James, to my wedded husband, to have and to hold from this day forward, for better for worse, for richer for poorer, in sickness and in health, to love and to cherish (*or* to love, cherish and to obey), till death us do part, according to God's holy ordinance; and thereto I give thee my troth.'

Again the bridal pair free their hands. The best man places the wedding ring upon the open prayer book held by the clergyman; and he then takes it and gives it to the bridegroom, to place on the third finger of the bride's left hand (earlier that morning she should move her engagement ring from the left hand to the right, leaving the ring-finger bare). Holding the ring in place, the bridegroom then repeats after the clergyman:

'With this ring I thee wed, with my body I thee worship, and with all my worldly goods I thee endow: In the Name of the Father, and of the Son, and of the Holy Ghost. Amen.'

If the bride wishes similarly to set a ring on her husband's finger, as is now quite often done, the bridal couple should discuss this with the clergyman in advance, and the exchange of rings takes place at this point.

Prayers for the constancy and love of the couple follow as they kneel. Joining their hands together, the clergyman utters the solemn words: 'Those whom God hath joined together let no man put asunder.' He then declares the marriage to the congregation, and the ceremony concludes with a blessing, a psalm and prayers.

The bridegroom then gives the bride his left arm and they proceed to the vestry, following the clergyman and followed by the chief bridesmaid with the best man, the parents of the happy couple, and perhaps grandparents. The register is signed, the bride using her maiden name for the last time. The bridal retinue re-forms for the recessional, and as the organist plays the Wedding March (the best man signalling to him when the procession is ready) the bride makes her way down the aisle on her bridegroom's left arm, her veil thrown back, with her attendants and her family following in pairs behind her, the bridegroom's father escorting the bride's mother, and the bride's father escorting the bridegroom's mother. This is the greatest moment of happiness and triumph for the radiant bride: one to be remembered and caught forever by the

110

photographers waiting outside as the bells ring out in the wedding peal.

And so to the reception, the best man being responsible for the organising of the cars: the first carrying the bride and groom, the second the parents of the bridal pair, and then, after a short pause to allow them time to reach the reception ahead of the guests, the bridesmaids, the grandparents, and so on, until all are away, the best man being the last to leave the church.

The Roman Catholic ceremony

'We publish the banns of marriage between Richard Joseph Mansell, of 1 Lufton Street, Barchester, and Teresa Mary O'Brien, of 17 Cathedral Lane, Barchester. Wherefore if any of you know of any impediment, whether of consanguinety, affinity, or spiritual relationship whereby these two persons may not be joined in marriage, you are to declare the same to us as soon as possible.'

A wedding according to the rites of the Roman Catholic Church can be celebrated in simple or solemn form. The simple form embraces the marriage service alone, the vows being made by the couple and blessed by the priest in the presence of at least two witnesses. This form of service is used for all marriages when for one reason or another the parties do not wish for Nuptial Mass. The solemn form, with Nuptial Mass (this may be High Mass, with three priests and a choir, or Low Mass, with or without music), is used when the parties wish it, even when one of them is not a Catholic.

There are certain conditions to 'mixed marriages'—that is, marriages between Roman Catholics and men or women who have been baptised or brought up in other faiths. It is usual for the non-Catholic to receive some instruction about the Catholic faith from the priest before the ceremony is performed, although this does not involve any pressure to convert. It is no longer obligatory for the non-Catholic to promise (but only to agree) that the children of the marriage shall be brought up in the Roman Catholic faith. Permission may also be granted for the marriage to take place in a non-Catholic church, and for ministers of other faiths to take some part in the ceremonies.

If the bride and groom are both Catholics, the service is preceded by the reading of the banns on three successive Sundays in the parish of each party. The couple must, however, still fulfil the legal formalities (pages 97–99).

In general, the arrangements follow the lines already described. It is no longer essential for women to cover their heads, although it is still courteous to do so. If Nuptial Mass is to be said, the bridal couple may like to choose two young altar servers, in addition to the usual bridal attendants.

When the bridal party is assembled, the bride on her father's right arm is led in procession to the Communion rail, where her bridegroom awaits her. The marriage service opens with a prayer, readings from Scripture, and a short homily. This is followed by an exchange of vows, the bridegroom and the bride consenting when asked if each will take the other in wedlock, and promising to be loyal and faithful to each other until death; these vows are the basis of the marriage contract.

The priest proclaims that the couple are joined together in marriage. The ceremonies of blessing and donning the ring then take place, the bridegroom saying 'Teresa, receive this ring as a sign of my love and fidelity, in the name of the Father and of the Son and of the Holy Spirit' and placing the ring on the third finger of his bride's left hand. If the bride wishes to bestow a ring on the groom, she does so at this point, having first discussed this with the priest; she uses the same words: 'Richard, receive this ring as a sign of my love and fidelity, in the name of the Father and of the Son and of the Holy Spirit.'

The civil declaration is incorporated into the marriage ceremony, and the words are said by the bridegroom and the bride in turn after the priest.

The bridal couple, attendants, witnesses and close relatives, proceed to the sacristy, as described on page 110, for the signing of the register.

At the conclusion of the ceremonies, the bride and bridegroom leave the sanctuary and, with their retinue re-formed, recess down the aisle to the church door; and so on to the reception.

A Free Church marriage

Couples wishing to marry according to the rites of the Free Churches—Baptist, Congregational, Methodist, Presbyterian, and other divisions of the Protestant faith—should consult their minister at least eight weeks prior to the date they hope to arrange for the ceremony. Most of the churches within these denominations are registered as buildings where marriages may be solemnised, just as the majority of their ministers have received sanction to conduct marriages as 'authorised persons' according to civil law; where a minister has not received such sanction, a registrar must be present to record the wedding, or a separate civil ceremony must have already taken place at a register office. The minister will advise the parties about the law's requirements (page 97) and will put them in touch with the local superintendent registrar(s) from whom the certificate, and if necessary licence, to marry (page 98) may be obtained.

Certain requirements are necessary to all Free Church marriages: the bride and groom should be at least sixteen, and if under eighteen should have parental consent; they must be unmarried or legally divorced (page 124); they must have given proper notice of their intention to marry, according to civil law; the service must take place in a registered building; the minister must be an 'authorised person', or the registrar must be present, or a separate civil ceremony must have already been conducted in a register office; at some point

112

in the service the bride and groom must each make a declaration in the presence of the 'authorised person' or the registrar—'I do solemnly declare that I know not of any lawful impediment why I, Charles Mason, may not be joined in matrimony to Anne Thatcher'—and must also say to each other in turn 'I call upon these persons here present to witness that I, Anne Thatcher, do take thee, Charles Mason, to my lawful wedded husband'; the bride and groom must both sign the marriage register, as should two witnesses in proof of the ceremony.

The degree of ceremonial at a Free Church wedding varies according to the denomination but the basic order of service, and the positions taken up by the bridal party, are on a line with those already described in the section on the Church of England wedding, as are the arrangements for the invitations, reception, and so on. The service opens with the betrothal; the minister again asks if there is any impediment to the marriage; the ring is blessed; the couple exchange vows; and the minister then blesses the marriage before the bridal party signs the register and reforms for the recessional.

The Quaker marriage

A wedding according to the usages of the Society of Friends is probably the simplest form of service to be found in any religious denomination. There is neither pomp nor ceremony; rarely wedding gown or top hat, seldom a best man or bridesmaids.

The formalities preceding the marriage must be strictly adhered to. At least six weeks in advance of the date proposed for the marriage, the couple must make application to the Registering Officer of the Monthly Meeting in whose compass the marriage is to take place (the names and addresses of Registering Officers are published by the Society in its annual Book of Meetings). The Registering Officer will supply all necessary forms. Form A requires a joint declaration of the intention to marry, with the proposed date and time of the marriage. If the Registering Officer assents to the application, he will arrange for public notice of the intended marriage to be given at the close of the meeting for worship at the Meeting House of which the parties are members, or which is nearest to their place of residence. If either of the parties is not a Friend, they will need to complete Form B (if a man) or Form C (if a woman), applying for permission to be married in accordance with the usages of the Society. Such application must be supported by the written recommendation of two adult members of the Society, who are expected first to discuss the application with the parties. The Registering Officer, if he assents to the application, will issue Form D, granting the couple permission to marry according to the Friends' usages. This form should then be taken to the superintendent registrar.

Responsibility for appointing a meeting for worship for the solemnisation of the marriage rests with the Monthly Meeting in whose area it is being held. The Registering Officer will take all the necessary steps.

The marriage takes place in a meeting for worship where, out of an atmosphere of expectant silent waiting on God, there is freedom of utterance, whether in ministry or prayer. At the appropriate moment, usually early in the meeting, the couple rise, hand in hand, to make their declaration of marriage, the man saying 'Friends, I take this my friend Rachel Brown to be my wife, promising through divine assistance to be her loving and faithful husband so long as we both on earth shall live' and the woman then making a similar declaration. A certificate of marriage is either signed then or towards the close of the meeting, by the bridal couple and by two witnesses, and is read aloud by the Registering Officer.

The close of the meeting is signified by the elders shaking hands. After the meeting, relatives, friends and guests usually add their signatures to the Certificate.

Although there may be an exchange of rings, this does not form part of the ceremony.

The Salvation Army marriage

Anyone contracting a marriage to a member of the Salvation Army is entering into a relationship with a man or woman who has undertaken special pledges and bound himself or herself to a disciplined life, and should, if possible, share or sympathise with those principles. The Corps Officer will advise the bride and groom whether the Army hall is registered for the solemnization of marriages and whether the registrar should be asked to attend there for the civil ceremony or a religious wedding be held following a civil ceremony at the register office. The usual legal formalities (pages 97–99) must be gone through.

Nowadays it is accepted that a non-Salvationist bride will marry in the traditional white gown and veil, if she so wishes, with attendants and flowers and music. If the bride and groom are both Salvationists, they may choose to marry in full uniform, the bride leaving off her bonnet if she prefers. There are no rules to govern the dress and bearing of non-Salvationist guests, the whole weight of Army tradition being 'Come as you are.'

At a full Salvationist wedding, the bride and groom will take their vows 'under the colours', the officer first reading out the six special articles which they must accept—a declaration that they have not sought the marriage for the sake of their own happiness and interests only, a promise that it will not lessen their devotion to God and their service in the Army, a promise to influence one another 'to promote our constant and entire self-sacrifice for the salvation of the world', a promise to make their home a place where all shall be aware of God

114

and to train up their children for His service, a promise to do their utmost to prevent injury or hindrance to God's cause, and a promise that if either ceases to be an efficient soldier the other will still continue to fulfil these undertakings as best he or she may.

The statement and the promise which follow are made by the groom and bride in turn, and are on the usual lines; each then makes the traditional declaration—'I, ——, do take thee, ——'—the wording used being similar to that of the Anglican Church, concluding 'And this I declare upon my honour, as a true soldier of Jesus Christ.' (The bride does not promise to obey.) The bridegroom sets a ring on her finger as a pledge, and she in turn may set one on his; and the officer then joins their right hands and declares the marriage.

If the bride and groom are not Salvationists, they may none the less be married by a Salvation Army officer. The articles are not read; but the statement, declaration and promise are made by each in turn, the ring or rings given in pledge, the hands joined and the marriage declared.

It is usual for the officer to say a short prayer, which may, if the couple are both Salvationists, be followed by a traditional 'volley' of Amens, before the couple proceed with the officer and their witnesses to sign the Register.

A humanist ceremony

A simple wedding ceremony is in use at the Humanist Centre, Conway Hall, London. This incorporates the declaration and promise required by law, as already mentioned in the section dealing with the civil ceremony (page 108), in a framework which can be varied to meet the wishes of the couple concerned. The officiant declares 'We come together to witness the joining of two lives,' and may then read a suitable short passage of prose or poetry. He speaks of love: 'When a man and a woman openly and sincerely declare their affection for each other they are affirming the precious truth that love is the foundation of all life: between man and woman, between parents and children, between relatives, between friends and, as goodwill, between all mankind. Hence we who are present here are witness not only to a legal act but also to a deeper truth. In the name of the community we represent we ask this man and this woman to speak in truth to one another and to repeat in the spirit of faithful engagement these words of solemn declaration that bind them together.' Following the declaration, the joining of hands, and the promise, the groom gives the bride a ring—and she, if she wishes, bestows a ring on him also—and may repeat the phrases from the Anglican ceremony beginning 'With this ring I thee wed—' They then say together, after the officiant, 'We have wed each other and do pledge ourselves in honour to prefer each other's good and to work together for the common good. We aspire to have and to hold together from this day

115

forwards for better or for worse, for richer or for poorer, in sickness and in health, and to love and to cherish as long as we may live.' The officiant pronounces them man and wife, and wishes them all the joy and happiness that mutual love may bring and a future of value and happiness for them and the world they live in.

Such a ceremony must include the declaration and promise as required by law, and must be performed by an 'authorised person' in a 'registered building', with the witnesses and under the conditions the law lays down. Couples interested in the possibility of being married in such a form may write to the South Place Ethical Society for details (page 155).

The Jewish marriage

Before a marriage can be solemnised according to Jewish rites, certain formalities must be observed. Application for authorisation must be made four to six weeks—not later than two weeks—in advance of the date proposed for the marriage. The parties should attend at the office of the Chief Rabbi (page 155), accompanied by a witness or witnesses—preferably one or more of the parents on both sides, or close relatives to whom the bride and bridegroom are known personally.

They should take with them the following documents:

1 The Certificate or Licence obtained from the superintendent registrar of marriages (see page 117)
2 The Jewish marriage lines of their respective parents or, if these are not available, the dates and places of the marriages
3 Their *full* birth certificates, showing the names of their parents and the dates of their births
4 Where there has been a change of name since the parents' marriage, documentary evidence of this
5 The Hebrew or Jewish names of the bride, the groom, and their fathers, and the information as to whether the bridegroom and the bride's father are Cohens, Levites or Israelites
6 If either party has been previously married, details about that marriage with evidence of death or, where applicable, of *get* (Jewish divorce)
7 Where one party is not of Jewish birth, evidence of proselytisation.

As there is frequently a large attendance at the office on Sundays, parties are advised to attend on weekdays if possible. Appointments can be made by telephone, except for Sunday mornings. People are asked to note that in all cases where further enquiries may be necessary—where documents have been issued abroad, for example, and so cannot be offered in evidence, or where applicants are resident abroad—the advice of the Chief Rabbi's Office should be sought without delay.

Some eight or ten weeks before the ceremony, the couple must attend at the office of the registrar of marriages in their district and state their intention of undergoing a Jewish wedding, giving details of the place and time. After a three-week period, the registrar will issue a certificate which must be taken to the Chief Rabbi's Office for the authorisation of Jewish Marriages.

In the synagogue the Secretary for Marriages has in his possession the Civil Registers. After the religious ceremony he will get the bride and the bridegroom to sign the Registers formally in the presence of two witnesses, who also sign. A copy of the marriage entry is usually given to the bridal couple: this is their civil marriage certificate, in addition to the religious marriage document given to them. The witnesses who sign the religious document are not the same as the witnesses who sign the civil one, being usually the two officiating members of the clergy.

Marriage according to Jewish rites requires that the bride and bridegroom are Jews and are free from any religious impediment to marry each other. The marriage may take place at any time except on the Jewish Sabbath and on certain feast and fast days. It is customary for the young couple to attend divine service with their respective fathers on the Sabbath prior to the wedding, and to fast on the day of the marriage so as to enter wedlock in a state of grace.

At a Jewish wedding, every member of the congregation must have his or her head covered. The bride wears a veil, a long-sleeved dress, and gloves. The bridegroom and all male members of the party wear evening dress—usually dinner suits.

The bridegroom arrives at the synagogue first, accompanied by his own father, the bride's father, and all male members of both families, and is conducted to his place under the canopy. The bride's procession consists of the bride herself on her father's right arm, with her bridesmaids, the bridegroom's parents, and her own mother, together with grandparents and relatives of both families; thus escorted, she is brought under the canopy to stand on the right of the bridegroom. The bridesmaids usually stand behind the bride and the other ladies of the party take their positions at her side, while the male members of the party range themselves at the side of the bridegroom. The clergy face the bride and bridegroom.

The service begins with a blessing of welcome and a psalm, followed by an address to the young people. The betrothal blessing given, the bridegroom then places the wedding ring on the second finger of the bride's hand, declaring 'Behold thou art consecrated unto me by this ring according to the law of Moses and Israel.' This declaration consecrates the marriage in the Orthodox synagogues, although in some synagogues there are variations of the service. The marriage contract is then read, in Aramaic and in English, and the seven benedictions are then chanted by the rabbi:

The Blessing over the cup of wine
The Praise of God as creator of the universe
                 as creator of man
                 as creator of mankind in His image
Prayers for the comfort of Zion
Prayer for the rejoicing of the young couple
Prayer for the couple's happiness and for the restoration of joy and gladness in the cities of Judah and in the streets of Jerusalem

A wineglass is then set under the bridegroom's heel and this he breaks, symbolising that in the midst of joy there is sorrow. The ceremony ends with the old blessing:

'The Lord bless you and keep you, the Lord make His face to shine upon you and be gracious unto you, the Lord lift up His countenance upon you and give you peace.'

The Muslim marriage

Those contemplating an Islamic marriage in Britain are advised by the Imam of the Islamic Cultural Centre in London that since it is necessary that all marriages taking place in Britain are recorded according to civil law, they should get in touch with their local superintendent registrar and arrange for a civil ceremony to precede that according to Islamic rites.

The law of Islam permits a Muslim man to marry a Christian or Jewish girl, and she is allowed to keep her own religion and freedom of worship. Nowadays many Muslim men are marrying British girls, but the main trend is still for Muslim to marry Muslim.

Normally a Muslim marriage is a simple ceremony which can be performed anywhere and need not necessarily be held in a mosque or in the presence of a minister of religion. Once the two parties concerned agree to marry, they then state their intention before a group of Muslims, two of whom should be males; from a religious point of view, they are then married. However, the usual procedure in Britain is for a civil ceremony to be held in a register office either on the day of, or a few days prior, a religious service in the mosque. This can be a simple quiet affair before two witnesses, or a ceremony with the full pomp and circumstances of any traditional wedding.

The text of the service is, in fact, an exchange of contracts. After praying to Allah, and praying for Allah's mercy upon the prophet Mohammed, the girl says to the man: 'I, ——, marry you according to Islamic Law in the presence of these witnesses with the dowry agreed upon, and Allah is our best witness.' The man replies: 'I, ——, accept marrying you to myself according to Islamic rites in the presence of the witnesses here with the dowry agreed upon, and Allah is our best witness.' In spite of its brevity and simplicity, the ceremony is moving, and the Imam's homily which follows stresses the need for understanding, compassion, faithfulness and deep love within the marriage, which must endure not only in this life but beyond.

It is interesting to note that the dowry is given by the man as a symbolic gesture. No need for a Women's Property Act: for the best part of fourteen hundred years, Islamic Law has decreed that on marriage a husband must protect his wife's future and that of his children; the act of marriage itself makes him completely responsible for their maintenance. In monetary terms, the dowry can be £5 or £5,000, but in either case the gesture symbolises the act. Another interesting feature is that although at the end of the ceremony a wish is expressed that the couple will be blessed with many children, no mention is made of marriage being primarily for the procreation of children, as is the case with the Anglican service; the stress is on the mutual comfort, compassion and love of the bride and the bridegroom.

At the end of the ceremony, a Certificate of Marriage will be issued by the Islamic Centre. The fee for this is independent of the registrar's charges for the civil ceremony.

Women attending Muslim marriages wear full-length dresses or trousers as the legs should be covered, as should the head and arms.

A Buddhist marriage

Buddhist marriages, which are considered to be private contracts between the two parties, require, in Great Britain as in most countries, civil registration, as already described on pages 97–99. Services of blessing, differing according to the country of origin, are conducted at the Thai, Sri Lanka and Tibetan religious establishments in this country, as well as at various Buddhist organisations. Details can be obtained by writing to the Buddhist Society, at the address given on page 155.

The reception

The reception is usually given by the bride's parents. Generally the guests go on from the church to the house or hall or restaurant where it is to be held, but occasionally the couple prefer to have a quiet wedding attended by immediate relatives and close friends only, followed by a large reception to which guests are invited (an example of an invitation for this type of reception appears on page 48).

The bride's parents should take up their stand in the ante-room or at the door of the room where the reception is to be held, in readiness to welcome their guests. The groom's parents should be invited to join the bride's parents, standing a little further in, to shake hands with the guests and to exchange a few pleasantries; introductions are made later on, when all the guests have been welcomed and the bride and bridegroom are mingling with the party. The young couple move towards the centre of the reception room to receive the good wishes and congratulations of their friends.

Seating arrangements follow a fairly orthodox plan if luncheon or any other form of sit-down meal is offered. The bridal pair sit together at the centre of the top table, with the bride on the groom's left. The wedding cake is in front of them. On the bride's left sits her father, then the groom's mother; on the groom's right sits the bride's mother, then his own father. The best man and the chief bridesmaid usually sit at the top table (the best man sitting next to the groom's mother, with the chief bridesmaid on his left and the second bridesmaid and chief usher to balance the seating at the other end of the table, or the chief bridesmaid sitting beside the groom's father, while the chief usher and the second bridesmaid sit at the second table). Grandparents should also sit at the top table, as should the clergyman if he is free to attend. The other bridesmaids, suitably partnered by young men, are at the lower tables, while other relations and friends of both families should mix as much as possible, each woman seated next to a man.

If the clergyman is present at the luncheon, the bride's mother should invite him to say Grace.

If the meal is a buffet laid out on long side-tables, the wedding cake is usually placed on a small separate table. Space is important at this kind of reception where guests are moving around, but a few chairs should be made available for the older members of the party, who should have first attention from those handing round the refreshments.

The speeches and toasts are nowadays few in number and brief in content and usually follow the ceremonial cutting of the cake by the bride and groom. It is usual for the bridal pair to cut the first slice, photographs being taken as they do so; the waiters then remove the cake to a side-table and cut small slices which are handed round to the guests, and glasses are charged for the toasts.

The bride's father or an old friend of the family proposes the first toast, speaking briefly and simply, perhaps on the following lines:

'Ladies and gentlemen, it is with great pleasure that I undertake the traditional duty of proposing the first toast to the happiness of these young people. As parents my wife and I are perhaps over-fond of our daughter, and to us this is a wonderful day, and we are delighted that so many relations and friends are here to share our joy. I therefore ask you to raise your glasses and drink with me the toast to John and Vivienne, to their health and happiness, and to their future prosperity.'

The bridegroom responds to this, beginning traditionally with the words 'My wife and I' ——

'My wife and I—how strange it sounds—thank you most sincerely for your good wishes. I am deeply conscious at this moment of my good fortune in having won Vivienne as my bride, and also in having acquired two extra parents who have treated me with such kindness that I feel almost guilty in robbing them of their daughter, though not quite guilty enough to prevent my doing so.  I would also like to thank my own parents for giving me a life full of happiness and opportunity enabling me to reach this happy status and to enter marriage secure in the knowledge that it is an enduring institution. Lastly I should like to thank Jane and Elizabeth, my wife's bridesmaids, who have so ably supported her through this day, and I ask you to join with me in drinking to their good health and happiness.'

The best man responds still more briefly on behalf of the bridesmaids, and this should bring the toasts and speeches to an end. He may then read out the congratulatory telegrams and greetings cards.

Throughout the reception the best man should keep a sharp eye on the clock to see that the bride and groom get away in good time for the honeymoon journey. Usually the bride goes upstairs to change soon after the final toast is drunk, with a sister or bridesmaid to help her. The best man should ensure that the car is waiting and the luggage loaded, preferably with a driver to defend it  from risqué guests. The groom slips away to change; the best man checks that all the tickets and travel documents are in the groom's safe-keeping; and the bridal couple then re-appear together. By tradition the bride throws her bouquet from the top of the stairs to the bridesmaids waiting below, the one who catches it supposedly being the next bride. She and the bridegroom then make their farewells, the bride kissing her parents and parents-in-law before running with the groom to the waiting car, showered with rice and rose petals.

And afterwards

If possible, the bride should leave a note of thanks for her parents and a small gift for her mother. Alternatively she and her husband may like to send flowers by Interflora to both mothers, before setting off on the honeymoon journey. It is courteous to write a brief note of thanks to the minister and perhaps one to the chief bridesmaid, and it is considerate to telephone or telegram both sets of parents to confirm safe arrival once the place of the honeymoon is reached; this done, there is nothing to do but be happy.

It is usual to send small slices of wedding cake to friends and relations who were unable to attend. The caterers may be willing to do this, given a list of names and addresses, but often the bride's mother prefers to send them out herself with the help of the bridesmaids, consulting with the groom's parents to be sure the list is complete.

Many families like to see a report of the wedding in the local paper. Telephone the paper in advance and see if they have a form for the bride's parents to complete and send in—they often do, as this guarantees that the details are correct—or if they would like a short report written by a member of the family, with or without a photograph, and if so, how long it should be.

The marriage took place at St Peter's Church, Barchester, on Saturday June 4, of Mr John James Reid, elder son of Mr and Mrs J. P. Reid of Barchester, and Miss Philippa Mary Wright, only daughter of Mr and Mrs K. Wright of Barchester. The service was conducted by Canon S. T. Johns and the organist was Mr M. Matthews. Given away by her father, the bride wore an ivory silk dress and her mother's lace wedding veil and carried a bouquet of white roses. She was attended by a page, James Reid, the bridegroom's youngest brother, in Highland dress, and three bridesmaids, Miss Emma-Jane Morgan, her god-daughter, Miss Elizabeth Reid, the bridegroom's sister, and Miss Anne Wright, her cousin, in French navy silk with posies of red roses. The best man was Mr Stephen Knight and the ushers were Mr Keith Reid, Mr David Morgan and Mr Guy Wright. A reception was held at the Royal Hotel in King's Square. The couple are spending their honeymoon in Paris.

Alternatively, a simple announcement may be sent to the newspaper:

Mr J. J. Reid, Miss P. M. Wright—On Saturday June 4, at St Peter's, Barchester, Mr John James Reid, elder son of Mr and Mrs J. P. Reid, to Miss Philippa Mary Wright, only daughter of Mr and Mrs K. Wright.

Special cases

The widow marries again

A widow is free to marry in church according to the rites of her religion. Proof of widowhood may be required when the arrangements for the wedding are being made.

The procedure is similar to that followed for a first wedding, except that the tone of the ceremony should be quiet and unostentatious. Guests at the church are usually limited to the immediate family and to a few close friends. A matron of honour usually replaces the bridesmaids, a charming outfit is chosen instead of the traditional wedding gown, a pretty hat worn instead of wreath and veil. The bride may like to carry a bouquet of pastel-coloured flowers or, more usually, to wear a spray of orchids or carry a prayer book or pochette. The altar can be simply decorated. The groom invites a friend to support him as best man, the bride asks her father or some other relative or close friend to escort her.

An older widow may like to issue her own invitations, but if she is still young her parents or friends are usually happy to undertake this for her. Throughout widowhood she continues to use her late husband's given name or initials—Mrs James Smith, Mrs J. P. Smith—and she should so be styled on the invitations to her second marriage.

A widow should remove her 'first' wedding ring the night before her second marriage. It should never be worn again.

Marriage to a widower

It is quite in order for a young bride marrying a widower to wear a white dress, a wreath and a veil, to have a full retinue of attendants, and to ask her father to give her away, and it is her prerogative to choose the place where the wedding is to be held, and, after the usual discussions with her bridegroom and her parents, the manner of service, the degree of formality, and the type of reception. It is, however, courteous to have a quieter, simpler wedding if the marriage is taking place fairly soon after the bereavement, and the bride should be considerate of the feelings of her groom's first 'in-laws' and in particular, of his children.

Marriage after divorce

In England and Wales civil law permits the marriage of divorced persons after the **decree absolute** has been granted. The decree absolute must not be confused with the **decree nisi,** which pronounces the divorce but does not free the parties to re-marry until the petitioner has applied for and been granted the decree absolute—usually about six weeks later. A superintendent registrar of marriages cannot refuse to marry divorced persons so long as a decree absolute is produced and there are no other legal impediments, and the marriage of divorced persons does accordingly usually take place in a register office, with the brief and simple civil ceremony. In Northern Ireland too the divorced may marry in a register office, once the decree absolute has been granted, which there is usually six months after the decree nisi.

The re-marriage of divorced persons is contrary to Church of England doctrine, but a person whose previous marriage has been declared null can marry in an Anglican Church. The Roman Catholic Church strictly forbids the re-marriage of the divorced, although where the first marriage did not comply with Church Law—if, for example, it was a civil ceremony held in a register office—the parish priest should be consulted—and indeed where there is reasonable doubt on any account. The Free Churches vary in their attitude; some give an adamant refusal, others will consider each case on its merits. The Society of Friends—the Quakers—give discretion to their Monthly Meetings to decide whether to grant permission to the divorced who wish to re-marry. The Church of Ireland's approach is very similar to the Anglican church.

Legally, a man or woman who has divorced or been divorced is still a divorcé or divorcée (sometimes called a *femme sole*), even if the former spouse dies following the decree. In such circumstances, however, it is generally possible to marry in church, having no former partner alive. At the time of application for a second marriage, the decree absolute and the death certificate should be produced, and the clergyman or registrar told of the position.

A decree of nullity in respect of a former marriage must be produced when an application is made to marry again in church.

Formerly the divorcée's wedding attire was a supposedly 'pretty' ensemble and a flowery hat, but nowadays wreaths and veils, white trouser suits, fur-edged robes, period costumes and hippie gowns jostle each other, and she is free to decide for herself, no longer bound by tradition or discretion.

The discretionary service of blessing following a civil marriage has already been mentioned on page 108.

There are many Christian people who, having contracted a civil marriage during the lifetime of a former partner, still feel the great need to take Holy Communion with their families, especially where there has been a long association with the church. In such instances, the incumbent or parish priest can present a case to the bishop of the diocese and he, having satisfied himself that the request is made in good faith and that the man or woman concerned would benefit from receiving the sacrament, can signify his approval; this approval, given in writing, is accepted as authoritative in that diocese and in all others within the province.

In Scotland there is no decree nisi. A decree of divorce or nullity granted by the Court of Session in Edinburgh is absolute and the party concerned is free to re-marry from the date of pronouncement, though it is open to the defender to lodge an appeal within twenty-one days of that date. Evidence of divorce or nullity must be produced to the registrar when giving notice of re-marriage or applying for the marriage schedule. A divorced partner who wishes to re-marry in church, or to have a service of blessing following a civil marriage, should ask their clergyman whether this will be possible.

'Marriage at sea'

Under English law, 'marriage at sea' does not exist. Ships are not registered for the solemnisation of marriages, and are outside the jurisdiction of the Archbishop of Canterbury's special licence. Men and women of British nationality contracting marriages on board ships registered under foreign flags would find them null and void on their return to this country.

Expenses

Wedding expenses can be varied according to circumstances, but generally are as follows: the bride's parents are responsible for press announcements, the printing of invitations and service sheets, the bride's dress and trousseau, the reception, with the wine and the wedding cake, flowers for the church and the reception, and cars taking the bride's party to the church. The bridegroom meets all church fees, the cost of the licence and the wedding ring, the bride's bouquet and those of the bridesmaids, and often pays for sprays or corsages for his mother and his bride's mother. He pays for the car which takes himself and his best man to the church, and for that in which he and his bride will drive from the church to the reception—and later, if necessary, to the station or airport for the start of the honeymoon journey. He presents modest gifts to the bridesmaids—lockets, perhaps, or bracelets for child bridesmaids—and gives his best man a small memento of the occasion. These are usually presented the day before the wedding, or on the morning of the day itself, so that they can be worn for the ceremony.

Shot-gun wedding expenses are better shared by both sets of parents. The young couple will need help in establishing themselves and the families should get together to see what can best be done to alleviate their position and to plan constructively for the immediate future. No need to get uptight either if the girl wants a white wedding—its symbolic significance was lost a long while ago.

Births, Adoptions, Christenings and Naming Ceremonies

The birth

> BLACK—on April 19 1974 at Park Royal Hospital, to Jane, wife of John Black, a son.

This kind of formal announcement appearing in national or local newspapers is history in the making for any family and calls for rejoicing and congratulations. The name or names of the child can appear in brackets at the end of the notice, though this is not strictly 'correct', or can be left for the informal printed notes which so many people now use as a means of letting friends know of the birth. Grandparents should receive the happy news from the father immediately, by telephone from the hospital if possible and certainly before any press announcement.

Congratulatory flowers, telegrams and letters should be acknowledged directly the mother feels able to do so, and as the stay in nursing home or hospital is now usually of brief duration, no doubt this will be when she reaches home. Bearing in mind that she may not be fully rested when she returns, visiting should be kept to a minimum during the first week.

In England, Wales and Northern Ireland, the birth must be registered within six weeks. If a member of the registrar's staff has not called at the hospital or clinic during the mother's stay, the father or mother must attend at the local office of the registrar of births, deaths and marriages as soon as possible. If the birth occurs **in Scotland,** it must be registered within three weeks. It can only be registered in a registration office—either that for the district in which the birth occurred, or that for the district in which the mother usually lives, if that is in Scotland.

The birth certificate

When a birth is registered, the registrar issues a shortened form of birth certificate which gives no details of parentage and which is acceptable for most purposes. This is issued free of charge (except in Northern Ireland where there is a fee). A certificate which shows full details of the birth may be obtained on payment of a fee.

A birth certificate must be kept safely as it is a much-needed document in later life, but if by any chance it is lost, or if for any reason further certificates are required, they can be obtained as described on page 151. When writing for full or short certificates, give as much information as possible, including the full name, the date and place of birth, and the full names of the parents.

Births at sea aboard British vessels are recorded by the master of the vessel and subsequently a record will be held by the Registrar-General of Shipping and Seamen.

Births in foreign countries may, in certain circumstances, be registered with the British Consul and, in some of the newly independent Commonwealth countries, with the British High Commission. Births occurring among families of members of H. M. forces serving outside the United Kingdom may be registered by the Service Department.

When the parents of an illegitimate child marry one another after the birth, the child is in most cases legitimated by the marriage and the birth can be re-registered in legitimate form. (This may be possible even if one parent has since died.) The legitimation of the child depends on the laws of the country of the father's domicile at the time of his marriage to the mother. **Re-registration** is free and when the new entry is made in the birth register, a new birth certificate can be obtained for the child, showing the parents' names exactly as though they had been married to one another when the child was born. These provisions are for England and Wales, but those for Scotland and Northern Ireland are substantially similar; application for re-registration should be made to the Registrar-General of the country in which the child was born.

Adoption

A court order is necessary to legalise an adoption. In England and Wales application should be made to the High Court (Family Division), the County Court or the Magistrates Court; in Scotland, to the Court of Session or Sherriff's Court; in Northern Ireland, to the High Court or County Court. All adoptions in the United Kingdom are registered in the Registers of Adopted Children, kept by the Registrars General, and certificates—including short certificates which contain no reference to adoption—can be obtained (pages 151–2).

Most newspapers have a special section for adoptions in their Personal columns. It is usual to insert a notice on the following lines:

> SMITH—on May 1 1974, by Elizabeth and John Smith, a son, now aged six months.

The adoptive parents may like to ask the newspaper to hold up the notice until it has one or two more so that the child, if it sees the notice in later years, will not feel too singled out.

Holy Baptism
Church of England

Although baptism in the Church of England often takes place when a child is quite small—a baby of a few weeks old, for example—it need not necessarily be conferred so early. There is a movement in favour of waiting until the child is old enough to understand the sacrament. Adult baptisms, preceding confirmation, are also fairly frequent.

If the child is being baptised, or—as people often say, 'christened'—as a baby, the ceremony is a family affair, usually confined to relatives and close friends. Formal invitations are rarely issued; instead, the mother usually sends out hand-written letters of invitation.

The godparents should be chosen before the date is fixed: two godmothers and one godfather for a girl; two godfathers and one godmother for a boy. (Godparents are not required in the Church of Scotland.) In the case of adult baptism, the man or woman concerned chooses his or her own sponsors. The Canon Law of the Church of England requires that a sponsor or godparent must have been baptised and confirmed, though the minister has the power to dispense with this requirement if he sees fit. In any case, it is important that those chosen are aware that whilst it is always a social honour to be asked to stand for a child, their undertaking is primarily of a spiritual nature and they should be prepared to take a little more than a material interest in its welfare. They should be close enough to the family to watch the child's development with real interest, and be prepared to offer friendship up to and after confirmation. Both godparents and parents should read through the service before the event so as to appreciate fully the significance of the promises which are to be made.

If a godparent is unable to attend the actual ceremony, a proxy of the same sex may be appointed to act for that day only.

The ceremony usually takes place on a Sunday, either after the children's service in the morning, or in the afternoon. Once the godparents have been appointed, the father of the child must approach the vicar who will officiate so as to arrange the time and date of the ceremony. If, for reasons of family and friendship, the parents would like to ask some other clergyman to take the ceremony, the vicar must be asked first. On the appointed day, the baby, probably in robe and veil, is taken to the church with parents and godparents in attendance. Relatives and friends not taking part in the actual ceremony will seat themselves in nearby pews while those directly concerned will group themselves round the font with the chief godmother on the left of the clergyman. At the commencement of the service she places the baby in his left arm and with the other godparents joins in the responses, at the appropriate moment stating clearly the name or names of the child. The clergyman then names the baby, making the sign of the cross with water on its brow. 'Julia, I baptise thee in the Name of the Father and of the Son and of the Holy Ghost.' With the conclusion of the baptism the infant is handed back to the godmother.

Before leaving the church, the father goes to the vestry and unobtrusively makes a donation to church funds whilst awaiting the issue of the Certificate of Baptism. Like the Birth Certificate, this is an important document which should be kept safely as it will be needed when the child is confirmed.

When a christening takes place after the morning service, it is customary to ask those who attend to **luncheon** and as normal courtesy the clergyman is invited. If his duties permit him to attend, he will say Grace before the meal.

When the christening takes place in the afternoon, **a simple tea** should be provided. The christening cake, decoratively iced with the baby's name and birthdate, occupies the centre of the table and it is cut by the mother immediately prior to the one toast—to the child's future. The toast can be drunk in champagne, or, with simplicity the order of the day, it is quite correct to provide only tea or soft drinks.

The range of **christening gifts** widens year by year and whether godparents are wealthy or of modest means, there is now a vast choice from small nursery needs to family plate. These can be sent by post or can be brought to the christening and put on display round the cake, or they can be presented to the parents personally and privately. The traditional gifts from godparents—silver mugs, tankards, a spoon and pusher, a silver rattle, a teething ring in ivory and silver, a thimble, a napkin ring, an egg cup and spoon, each suitably inscribed—remain ever-popular, but many, looking ahead, prefer to give a beautifully bound Bible or prayer book, or an encyclopaedia. Antique silver spoons, cutlery or exquisite glass from standard designs which can be added to over the years are becoming established favourites, while there is a growing trend towards National Savings Certificates, Premium or Property Bonds, since most of these will increase in value over a long term.

But this is the baby's day and as he is yet too young to be spoiled by admiration, it can be given in full to the joy of the proud parents.

A service of naming and blessing
At a time when it has become less automatic for parents to present their children for baptism, and when the clergy themselves are becoming more reluctant to baptise the children of non-practising Christians, a new form of service has come into being, which while not generally acceptable throughout the Church of England as a whole in its present form, is in use in some dioceses and does offer some solution to those parents who do not subscribe wholeheartedly to the Church on the subject of infant baptism, but want some

measure of recognition for their children as potential members of the Christian family. A Service of Naming and Blessing is in use at Chelmsford and another is in use at Southwark. A great deal depends upon whether the local bishop wishes to encourage the use of the service as opposed to baptism proper, or as a preliminary to baptism proper.

Those thinking men and women who are much perplexed on this matter might find it helpful to get in touch with their local bishop. They might also like to read a small booklet published by Grove Books entitled A SERVICE OF THANKSGIVING AND BLESSING by C. H. B. Byworth and J. A. Simpson.

The Roman Catholic baptism ceremony

Children are usually baptised in the Church of Rome fairly soon after birth and in the church of the father's parish. Two godparents are chosen, one of each sex; these ought to be practising Catholics aged fourteen or over. It is usual for at least one of the names chosen to be a saint's name. The baptism may be a quiet ceremony attended by the family and friends, or may take place during Holy Mass on Sunday, to welcome the child into the parish and into the Church.

On the chosen day, the baby is brought to the church by the parents and godparents, who are received by the priest. He greets those present, asks what name the child is to be given, and ask what they want of God's Church for the child—'Baptism.' He then reminds the parents of the responsibility they incur in presenting the child for baptism, ensures that they understand the significance of the rites, and asks the godparents whether they are prepared to assist the parents in their Christian duty. He then welcomes the child:

'Helena Mary, the Christian community welcomes you with great joy. In its name I claim you for Christ our Saviour by the sign of His cross. I now trace the cross on your forehead, and invite your parents and godparents to do the same.'

A Gospel passage is read, a short homily given, and bidding prayers said. The saints are invoked by name—the Virgin Mary, St John the Baptist, St Joseph, St Peter and St Paul (others being included if this is desired) and the saint or saints whose name the child bears: 'St Helena, pray for us.' The celebrant then reads the prayer of Exorcism and Anointing, and anoints the child on the breast with oil, the mother or godmother undoing its shawls and robe for the purpose. The group may then move to the baptistery, where the celebrant asks God to give the child new life in abundance through water and the Holy Spirit, blesses the water, and invokes God. The Renunciation of Sin and the Profession of Faith follow, and the celebrant then invites the parents and godparents to gather round the font and asks them whether it is their will that the child be baptised in the Faith. They reply, 'It is', and the child is baptised with water in the name of the Father and of the Son and of the Holy Spirit. The celebrant says

130

a short prayer and then anoints the child with the sacred chrism, in silence.

The baby is then 'clothed' with a white garment brought by the parents—a white shawl which may be wrapped around it, a white lace handkerchief to tuck over its breast, or anything else that is suitable—to symbolise that it is newly created and clothed in Christian dignity. A candle is lit for the child, if possible from the flame of the Easter candle, and the celebrant entrusts the parents and godparents with the task of keeping the flame of faith alive in the child's heart. Touching the child's ears and mouth with his thumb, he says the Ephphetha—'The Lord Jesus made the deaf hear and the dumb speak. May He soon touch your ears to receive His word, and your mouth to proclaim His faith, to the praise and glory of God the Father'—and then addresses the congregation, calling them to join with him in the Our Father. He then blesses first the mother, who holds the child; then the father; and then all those present.

The Society of Friends
The Friends have no formal naming ceremony, but it is usual for a baby to be welcomed into a meeting for worship soon after his birth, and Friends from the meeting are often appointed to visit parents on the birth of a child.

The dedication of a child—Salvation Army
If the parents of the child are both Salvationists, or if one is a Salvationist and the other accepts his or her resolve to train up the child for God's service, they may present their child to the Lord in a dedication service, which usually takes place towards the end of a morning or afternoon meeting. The child is usually simply dressed for this ceremony. The leader explains and declares the promises the parents are making, and they respond 'We are willing.' If any other children of the family are present, the officer may ask them if they will help their brother or sister to love God; and they answer, 'We will.' The congregation stands in prayer, and the officer then raises the child in his arms and using its full name, says 'Loving Heavenly Father, take this child, Michael William Smith, to be Thine own.' He formally accepts the child, 'fully given up by his parents for the salvation of the world', and charges the parents to keep their promise. A traditional 'volley' of Amens may follow, and a prayer. The parents sign the Dedication Register, and receive an official Certificate.

Non-Salvationists who wish to dedicate their child to God may do so, if at least one of them is resolved to train the child for God's service.

Jewish circumcision
All male children of Jewish parentage should be circumcised at the eighth day of their lives. The ceremony usually takes place in hospital or at home—rarely in

131

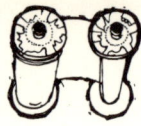

the synagogue. There are two sponsors—usually a married couple—together with parents, grandparents and a limited number of friends in attendance, although women, including the mother, are not usually present at the actual ceremony of circumcision.

On arrival, the father and male sponsor or godfather, called the *Sandek,* take the child into the room where he is to be initiated into the Covenant of Abraham and those present rise and say: 'Blessed be he that cometh.'

The father then states:

'I am here to perform the affirmative precept to circumcise my son, even as the Creator, blessed be he, hath commanded us, as it is written in the Law, that he that is eight days old shall be circumcised among you, every male throughout your generations.'

The *Mohel,* who is the person who does the circumcision, then takes the child and says a prayer, those present responding: 'O let us be satisfied with the goodness of thy house, thy holy temple.' Whereupon he places the child upon the knees of the *Sandek,* saying the following blessing:—

'Blessed art thou, O Lord our God, King of the universe, who has sanctified us by thy commandments, and has commanded us concerning the Circumcision.'

The circumcision is then performed and immediately the father says the blessing: 'Blessed art thou, O Lord our God, King of the Universe, who has sanctified us by thy commandments, and has commanded us to make our sons enter into the Covenant of Abraham our Father.' Those present respond:

'Even as the child has entered into the covenant, so may he enter into the Law, the nuptial canopy, and into good deeds.'

The *Mohel* continues in prayer, ending with the words: 'This little child, Benjamin (*or whatever name is chosen*), may he become great. Even as he has entered into the covenant, so may he enter into the Law, the nuptial canopy, and into good deeds.'

The *Sandek* drinks the wine from the Cup of Blessing, a few drops being given to the child; and then the Cup is sent to the mother, and she also partakes.

A Muslim naming ceremony

The tradition put forward by the Prophet is that a Muslim child should be given 'a good name' on the seventh day after birth. The ordinary call to prayer is recited in his ears in a soft voice. Such practices as *Aqiqa*—the killing of a sheep and distributing it as an act of charity—or cutting the hair, weighing it with gold and giving an equal amount in money to the poor, are also traditionally recommended.

132

Bereavement

Death inevitably shocks the nerve centre of every family and for those immediately concerned, awed by the sudden gulf between the finite and the infinite, and shattered by its seeming finality, the sense of loss and desolation is absolute. In these circumstances, no matter what swift practical measures are necessary, compassion must be uppermost in the minds of those dealing with the bereaved and they should be shown every possible kindness and consideration. Those outside the family circle should endeavour to convey their sympathy without intruding upon the private grief of individuals.

Taking charge

If death occurs in hospital, the authorities will take charge, calling a doctor if one is not presently in attendance and informing the next-of-kin. The nursing staff usually carry out the first offices for the dead. The hospital may want to carry out a post mortem, and if so will ask the next-of-kin if he or she will give signed consent to this. They will need to know whether cremation or burial is desired (pages 135–6).

If, however, death occurs at home, the first duty is usually to telephone the doctor—assuming, that is, that he is not already in attendance. He will need to know whether burial or cremation is desired—there are more details about this on page 135—as there are different statutory requirements for each. If the death is the result of an accident, or seems at all suspicious, leave everything exactly as it is, and call the police and the doctor at once.

If the deceased was a Roman Catholic it is customary to call the local priest at once (look in the local telephone directory under *Catholic Churches*) to give the last rites, unless this has been done before death.

The next step is usually to contact a funeral director. Ask the doctor whether there is a local firm, or look in the Yellow Pages of the telephone book. The funeral director will arrange for the first offices for the dead, if this has not already been done, and will carry out most of the painful formalities connected with death and interment or cremation. He can, and will if asked to do so, make himself responsible for all the following: announcing the death, escorting the person who is to register the death to the registrar's office, obtaining all necessary certificates, preparing the body, arranging for the service, printing and collecting Order of Service leaflets, receiving and listing wreaths and flowers, providing transport for the mourners, contacting solicitors, employers and others who must be informed of the death. In no way will he seek to usurp another's duties, but his experience and dignified efficiency will ease the burden for all concerned.

Announcing the death

The family and any close relatives should be informed immediately by telephone or telegram, and obituary notices dispatched or telephoned in time to appear in local and/or national newspapers the next day. If they are sent by post they must be signed by a relative or executor, unless sent in by a funeral director, or a solicitor, or received from another paper; if they are dictated over the telephone, the subscriber must give his name and address and number as confirmation, and will be telephoned back as a check.

Such notices are factual. As will be seen from the newspaper obituary columns, they are usually confined to the surname (as the heading); when, sometimes how (*As a result of an accident*—), and where death occurred (the name of a hospital or nursing home should not be given without permission); to whom (*Mary Jones, Captain James Smith R.N.*), and at what age if the next-of-kin wish to include this; the home address; relationship to surviving members of the family; and the funeral arrangements—the place, day and time of the service, the place of burial or cremation, requests for letters or mourning (*No letters, no mourning by his request*), arrangements re receipt of flowers, and whether there is to be a memorial service (*A memorial service will be held later, details to be announced*).

> JONES—On March 24 1974, at Birch Hall, Barchester, Mary Rose, beloved wife of Henry and mother of Joan and David. Funeral service at St John's Church on Thursday March 26 at 11 a.m., followed by private cremation. Family flowers only.

> SMITH—On April 2 1974 at a nursing home, Nigel H. Smith, aged 48, of Crestwood Grange, Buxted. Funeral at Crestwood Parish Church, Friday April 5 at 12 noon. Flowers to Fuller & Scott, The Wakelyne, Uckfield, or donations to Cancer Research.

Registering the death—England and Wales

The registrar

A death must normally be registered by an 'informant' within five days at the office of the registrar of births, deaths and marriages in whose sub-district it occurred. The funeral director will know the address (or it can be found in the telephone directory under *Registration,* and is also displayed in post offices, doctors' surgeries, and so on) and can if wished escort the next-of-kin there. The body cannot be buried or cremated until the registrar has issued a disposal certificate.

The registrar will need to see **the medical certificate of cause of death** which is issued by the doctor who was in attendance during the last illness or who was called after death. The doctor may post this certificate to the registrar himself and hand **a notice to informant** to the next-of-kin or to a similarly responsible person who is to act as the 'informant', or he may hand the certificate to the informant together with the notice. If the doctor feels he cannot issue a medical certificate—as might for instance be the case if he had not recently attended the deceased—or if the certificate he issues indicates to the registrar that death was the result of an accident, or that the deceased person was not attended by a doctor during his last illness, or, for various other reasons, that the death should be investigated further, the registrar will report the death to **the coroner,** initiating the procedure described in the next section. If death occurred in hospital, the doctor there will normally issue the certificate.

Assuming, however, that a straightforward medical certificate has been received by the registrar, and that he is satisfied by it, he will then register the death.

A qualified 'informant', usually a relative, must attend, to provide the registrar with the personal details which have to be entered in the register. If you act as an informant, you will be asked where death took place, the names of the deceased, sex, age, address, occupation, date and place of birth, and other questions varying according to the age and marital status of the person who has died. The registrar will ask the informant to check and sign the register entry. He will want to collect the deceased's medical card if it is available, so take this along. If the deceased had been receiving a pension or allowance from Government funds (other than the National Insurance Scheme), you should take the pension or allowance documents to the registrar too. Make a note of the number of any document before you surrender it.

For information about **death certificates**—that is, copies of the entry in the death register—see pages 139 and 151–2.

The registrar now issues **a disposal certificate.** If the deceased wished his body to be buried, or if he expressed no particular wish and burial is the choice of his next-of-kin, this certificate authorises burial. To save the next-of-kin anxiety, it is best for anyone preferring burial to leave a written statement to this effect (and this must then be honoured). It may be, however, that the deceased person preferred cremation to burial or, if he expressed no particular wish, that this is the family's preference. It is again best and simplest, and spares the bereaved worry about the last wishes of the dead, for anyone who wishes to be cremated after death to leave a short declaration in writing with the next-of-kin, legal representative or executor (don't rely on setting down such wishes in a Will, which may not be opened until after the funeral).

There are statutory requirements to be dealt with before cremation can take place. The funeral director can guide you through the regulations. **The application for cremation** must be completed by an executor or the nearest relative of the deceased, and counter-signed. A certificate must be completed by the doctor who has been attending the deceased, and a confirmatory medical certificate be completed by a registered medical practitioner of not less than five years' standing, who must not be a relative of the deceased, nor a relative or partner of the first doctor. Both must see the body. These forms are sent to the medical referee of the crematorium who will normally then issue **the authority to cremate.** If he feels he cannot do so, he may order a post mortem or report the death to the coroner.

Once the registrar's disposal certificate has been issued, the final preparations for the funeral can be made. If death occurred in hospital, the funeral director will make the arrangements for collecting the body (most hospitals have specific times for this), showing the registrar's certificate and an **authority to remove** signed by a relative of the deceased, and will convey it to a chapel of rest or, if the relatives prefer, to the family home.

The coroner

When a death is reported to the coroner, whether by the registrar, the medical referee, or anyone else, the family must accept that all control over, and responsibility for, the body passes from them to him or his officers. A constable is usually chosen by the Police Authority to act as a coroner's officer, and it is his duty to report on the circumstances of the death to the coroner.

If a doctor was in attendance on the deceased, he will contact him. He will also want to talk to the relatives, and it is their duty to answer all his questions as fully as they can and to tell him of any circumstances which might make it necessary for an inquest to be held.

If the next-of-kin wish to cremate the body, they should let the coroner know this in advance.

The coroner may decide that it is unnecessary to hold a post mortem or an inquest, and if so he will issue **a formal notification,** which allows the registrar to proceed with the registering of the death and the issue of the disposal certificate. The coroner does not have to inform the next-of-kin of his decision, and they should accordingly keep in touch with the registrar so that a qualified informant can attend before him to give the necessary details which are required for the death to be registered, and to sign the register.

The coroner may order **a post mortem** examination, which will be carried out by a medical practitioner. On seeing the findings the coroner may be satisfied, and indeed often is, that an inquest is unnecessary. In this case he sends the registrar **a certificate** stating the cause of death. The next-of-kin should keep in touch with the registrar. The coroner will indicate to the registrar whether he has issued **a certificate-for-cremation;** if he has, the registrar will not issue a certificate for disposal, but a qualified informant must still attend at the registrar's office, as described on page 135, to provide the information he requires and to sign the register. If, however, the body is to be buried, or if the coroner has not issued a certificate for cremation, the registrar will issue **a certificate for disposal.**

Alternatively the coroner may order **an inquest**—an official enquiry into the identity of the deceased and the causes and circumstances of his death, and, if necessary, the identification of the body.

After this hearing he will normally issue an **order for burial,** or if cremation is desired and he has been given prior notice of this, a **certificate-for-cremation.** These certificates are usually handed to relatives at the close of an inquest. A **report** on the findings of the inquest is sent by the coroner to the registrar, who will then register the death from the details supplied by the coroner. An informant is not required in this case.

In some cases, notably where death is the result of an accident, the coroner will open an inquest, to facilitate the carrying out of the funeral arrangements, and after a brief hearing will adjourn it to await statements from witnesses who have themselves been injured. In such circumstances he will usually issue an order for burial before he adjourns the hearing; he can only issue a certificate-for-cremation at such a hearing, however, in the case of death resulting from industrial, railway, flying or road accidents. This procedure does not apply to a case in which a criminal charge has been made.

Scotland

In Scotland a death must be registered within eight days, either at the office for the district in which it occurred, or at the office for the district in which the deceased usually resided. The informant should take with him the deceased's medical card and, where applicable, evidence that he or she was in receipt of a pension from public funds. He will be asked to answer the same basic questions as are listed on page 135, and will also be asked for the time of death, the date and place of birth, details about the spouse (and any former spouses), details about the parents. The registrar will need **the medical certificate of cause of death,** or the name and address of the doctor who can be asked for it. Lacking a satisfactory certificate, the registrar can still register the death, but must report the case to the procurator fiscal. The procurator fiscal with the aid of the police will

investigate the circumstances and may apply to the sheriff for a warrant to hold a post mortem. If there is a case for a public inquiry, the procurator fiscal will report this to the Lord Advocate, who decides whether to order an inquiry, held before a sherriff and a jury. The procurator fiscal informs the Registrar-General of the results of his enquiries and the Registrar-General takes whatever steps are necessary to have the death registration corrected or completed.

After registration, the registrar issues **a certificate of registration of death** which is required by the keeper of the burial ground or by the person in charge of the crematorium. **A National Insurance certificate** of registration of death is also usually issued to enable the next-of-kin to obtain the death grant. Both are issued free of charge. An extract of the entry in the register of deaths can be obtained for a fee (at present, 50p for the first extract, and 30p for second or subsequent extracts issued at the same time).

Northern Ireland

In Northern Ireland a death must normally be registered within five days, either at the office for the district in which it occurred or at the office for the district in which the deceased person resided. If **a medical certificate of cause of death** has been issued by the doctor who was in attendance during the last illness, the qualified informant, usually a relative, should take this along to the registrar's office, together with the deceased person's medical card and, if the deceased had been receiving a pension or allowance from Government funds (other than the National Insurance Scheme), any relevant documents. The informant will be asked to answer the usual basic questions (page 135). After registration of the death, the registrar issues **a certificate** which must be shown to the person in charge of the burial ground or, if cremation is preferred, the crematorium. He also issues **a National Insurance certificate** of registration of death, to enable the next-of-kin to claim the death grant.

If the death has been reported to the coroner, he will issue **his authority** for burial or cremation, but the death cannot be registered until the coroner has issued either **a notification** that he does not consider it necessary to hold an inquest, or his **certificate after inquest.**

If an inquest is held, the registrar will register the death from the details supplied by the coroner, and it is not necessary for an informant to attend at his office.

Copies of the entry in the register—**death certificates**—can be obtained from the registrar immediately after registration, or, in the week following registration, from the General Register Office, on payment of a fee.

The death grant

A standard grant, which at the present time is £30 maximum, may be payable on the death of an insured person if the National Insurance contribution conditions have been fulfilled. If they have been only partially fulfilled, a reduced grant may be payable. Women aged eighteen or over, born on or after July 5 1888, and men aged eighteen or over, born on or after July 5 1883, are eligible.

The death grant is usually paid to the executors, or to the administrators. It is usually issued in the form of a Giro order which can be cashed at a post office. It is not subject to estate duty.

Anyone wishing to claim this grant should do so within six months of the death, calling at the local office of Social Security. They should usually take with them the **special type of death certificate** for this purpose which will be issued free of charge by the registrar, the deceased's National Insurance contribution card, birth certificate, the marriage certificate where this is appropriate, any order books issued by the Department of Health and Social Security or any welfare food service books which relate to the deceased, and, if the claim is based on the payment of, or the intent now to pay, the funeral expenses, the undertaker's account or estimate.

A number of other useful leaflets are issued by the Department of Health and Social Security, and these are listed on page 148.

The funeral arrangements

Once the announcements have been made and the death registered and the certificates issued, the funeral director will see to **the final preparation** of the body. (If the next-of-kin do not want the body embalmed, they should make this clear from the start.) Some families like the dead to lie in their own home, others prefer to arrange with the funeral director for the use of a chapel of rest. In either case friends may wish to pay, briefly, their last respects before the funeral or cremation service, and may be told, if so, what time will be appropriate.

It is customary to have some form of religious service at a funeral, but it is not essential. Churchyard burial can take place without religious rites if the incumbent agrees, as can burial in a cemetery or cremation at a crematorium. A quiet and dignified non-religious ceremony can usually be held if desired. The British Humanist Association in London will advise you on this. They can also sometimes help with the provision of funeral officiants, though this depends a little on the area. Anyone anxious to be buried or cremated without a religious ceremony should make their wish plain, setting it down in writing well in advance (though in law this would not necessarily be binding on the next-of-kin), and the next-of-kin should advise the funeral director so that he can arrange for this with church, cemetery or crematorium authorities.

Usually, however, a religious service is held. In consultation with the funeral director and the minister who is to hold the funeral service, whether at the crematorium or at the church, the relatives may decide on the wording of the **Orders of Service,** if these are to be used (most churches and crematoria will provide hymnals, prayer books, and printed booklets, but many families like to have specially printed service sheets, bearing the full name and the date of death), and what **music** is to be played, what hymns sung and what psalms. The organist and choir should be booked, if this is desired. The funeral director will seek to avoid the embarrassing situation which arises when a small group of mourners under emotional stress try to struggle unaccompanied through hymns or psalms in a large church. Some crematoria chapels have a manual organ, but in many cases they rely on recorded music and have available a selection of tape and disc music from which the family can make its choice. If a church service is to be held, the choice of music is of course subject to the incumbent's approval. Favourite hymns are *Abide With Me, Eternal Father Strong to Save, For All The Saints, Jesus Lives, Lead Kindly Light, Love Divine All Loves Excelling, Nearer My God To Thee, Now The Day Is Over, O God Our Help In Ages Past, O Jesus I Have Promised, O Perfect Love, Rock of Ages, Take My Life And Let It Be, The Day Thou Gavest Lord Is Ended* and *Thine For Ever God Of Love.* Favourite psalms are number 23, *The Lord is my shepherd;* number 39, *I said I will take heed of my ways;* number 90, *Lord, thou hast been our refuge;* number 121, *I will lift up mine eyes unto the hills;* and number 130, *Out of the deep have I called unto thee, O Lord.*

Suitable voluntaries include Handel's *Largo* and *He shall feed his flock,* and his *I know that my Redeemer liveth;* Bach's *Air on a G String,* his *Jesu, joy of man's desiring,* and his *Sheep may safely graze;* Tchaikovsky's *Chanson Triste; Ave Maria,* either the Schubert setting or the Bach-Gounod; Chopin's *Funeral March; Nimrod,* from Elgar's *Enigma Variations;* the Brahms *Lullaby;* Beethoven's *Sonata Pathetique;* Walford Davies's setting of the brief and simple prayer *God be in my head;* the largo from Dvořák's *New World Symphony;* and Mendelssohn's *O rest in the Lord.*

If burial has been decided upon, arrangements will also be made for the obtaining and preparation of **a grave.** The funeral director will see to these after consultation with the family. It is sometimes possible to re-open an earlier grave so that husband and wife or mother and child may be buried together, and if this is what the family desires, he will discover whether it can be done. All Anglican parish churchyards in Great Britain are under the control of the Established Church, although their use is normally available to other Christians. Alternatively burial may take place in a cemetery.

Wreaths and fresh flowers should be sent to the house, or more usually, to the undertaker's, on the morning of the funeral. It is no longer customary to send all-white flowers. A plain card bearing the sender's name and a short message of sympathy should be attached, the degree of intimacy dictating the wording. Close relatives might write *With deepest affection* or *With all our love* or *With love and in affectionate memory;* friends and acquaintances *With deepest sympathy* or *In affectionate remembrance.* It is helpful to add one's full name on the reverse of the card, and to state the deceased's full name clearly. Family flowers only are placed on the coffin.

Deep mourning is seldom seen nowadays except where the deceased has held high office. Men of the immediate family usually wear sober suits and black ties, while other men attending wear black ties with ordinary lounge suits. Black armbands are usually worn only by members of the Services. Women should be quietly dressed and, as a small courtesy may like to wear hats or headscarves.

It is usual for members of the immediate family to gather at the house while other relatives and friends go direct to the church or crematorium. The cars carrying the immediate family form the cortège which follows the hearse to the place where the service is to be held.

The funeral director will supply the coffin-bearers. If the service is taking place in church, the minister will usually meet the coffin at the churchyard gate or at the church door and will read the 'opening sentence'—Verses 25 and 26 of the eleventh chapter of St John's Gospel are often chosen—and the coffin will be borne into the church, any relatives and friends who have gathered there rising to their feet as it is carried in, and the chief mourners following behind in procession. A widow or widower follows the coffin with the eldest son or daughter, the other children and sons- or daughters-in-law behind them, and then parents, brothers and sisters, and other relatives, colleagues and friends. Parents attending the funeral of a child walk together immediately after the coffin, their other children behind them, and then the grandparents, uncles and aunts. A childless widow following her husband's coffin should be escorted by a brother or other close relative or a close family friend. The coffin is placed in the chancel, or at the foot of the chancel steps, and the immediate relatives take their places in the front pews on the right.

If the service is taking place in a crematorium chapel, the other mourners will usually gather in the waiting room until the cortège arrives, and then follow the minister, the coffin and the chief mourners into the chapel.

The service and the committal

Funeral services differ according to the faith of the deceased, and the preferences of the family.

Christian

The authorised form of the **Anglican** service may be found in the Book of Common Prayer. The revision approved by the Church in 1928, though rejected by Parliament, is generally adopted in churches and chapels of the Established Church throughout Great Britain. When the coffin is in position and the mourners have taken their places, a psalm is read, followed by a lesson; the Lord's Pray is said; versicles and responses; a series of set prayers; and the blessing. This is the general outline of the service: hymns and psalms chosen by the family are generally included, however, and if a fully choral service is decided upon, it will be arranged to include an anthem, opening and closing voluntaries, and, frequently the *Nunc Dimittis* as the procession leaves. The committal prayers are said at the graveside, the coffin is lowered, and earth is cast three times upon it at the words 'Earth to earth, ashes to ashes, dust to dust'—this is usually done by a church official, but the funeral director may take on this duty. In Scotland mourners may be invited beforehand to hold a 'courtesy cord' at the committal.

If the ceremony of committal takes place in the churchyard, it is usual for the mourners to group themselves around the grave, with the immediate family standing closest to the graveside. If, however, the committal is to take place at some other cemetery, or private cremation is to follow, it is usual for relatives and close friends to follow the coffin out of the church and to join the cortège while the rest of the mourners rise to their feet and remain standing until the procession has driven away.

The Order of Service used in crematoria chapels is very similar, except that the congregation remains in the chapel for the whole of the service, including the committal prayers, in which the words 'We therefore commit this body to the elements (*or* to the flames), ashes to ashes, dust to dust' are used; it is at this moment that the curtains usually close slowly around the coffin as it moves towards the committal chamber. After a brief silent pause the mourners leave the chapel, usually shaking hands with the minister at the door. At most crematoria the wreaths and flowers are set out in a cloister beyond the chapel, with a sign bearing the name of the deceased, and the mourners walk quietly

past these, speak briefly to one of the chief mourners, and then depart.

At a **Roman Catholic** funeral; it is usual for a special requiem Mass to be said. Relatives and friends will often have other Masses said for the soul of the deceased, before and after burial.

For an **Anglo-Catholic** funeral, as for a Roman Catholic one, the coffin often rests in the church overnight. Candlesticks holding white candles are placed around it, and a pall may be used. A requiem Communion may be celebrated before the funeral.

Funerals according to the rites of the **Free Churches** are usually simple, but prayers and hymns and an address form a normal part of the service.

The funeral of a member of the Society of Friends is marked by particular simplicity. A Friend is usually appointed by each Monthly Meeting to co-ordinate arrangements for funerals. A Quaker funeral service takes the form of a silent meeting for worship, whether it is held in a crematorium chapel or in a Friends Meeting House. The meeting is usually closed by the Friends responsible shaking hands.

The **Salvation Army** funeral is traditionally a simple affair designed to display the triumph of faith over sorrow. The relatives of a deceased Salvationist should contact the local Corps so that an officer may conduct the arrangements, in consultation with the family and the undertaker. Non-Salvationists invited to attend need not necessarily wear mourning, and it is best to check in advance whether there will be flowers, or whether donations to the Army funds or some other charity are preferred. At a full Salvationist funeral, with Army honours, the colours will be spread on the coffin, and a march to the cemetery, led by the band, may take place. A special prayer of committal is normally said at the graveside, in the crematorium, or at the disposal of ashes after cremation. There are also special committal prayers which a Salvation Army officer may say, if wished, at the funeral of a non-Salvationist.

Jewish

On the death of a member of the Jewish faith, the funeral arrangements will usually be made by the synagogue to which he or she belonged. If the deceased had lost touch with the synagogue, his family or executors should contact the local synagogue or the local Jewish burial society.

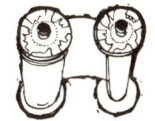

A Jewish funeral is predominantly a male affair, and usually only men will attend. A plain wooden coffin is used. All those present should cover their heads.

It is not usual to send flowers, but condolence cards and messages of sympathy may be sent to the bereaved.

Muslim

On the death of a Muslim, the face of the dead should be turned towards Mecca. It is usual for the first offices to be carried out by Muslims of the same sex as the dead, but if this is not possible a nurse or a professional person may see to their performance. The body must be handled with reverence and gentleness at all

times. Friends may be invited to see the body after death.

The funeral is arranged to take place as soon as possible after death. It is customary to inform the nearest Muslim community so that an Imam can conduct the funeral prayer, although, if none is available, any worthy Muslim may recite the prayers. Cremation is not a Muslim habit or tradition; a Muslim body will be buried. The grave should run north-west to south-east, so that the body faces Mecca, and although in many cases this is not possible some cemeteries provide special facilities for Muslim graves. The funeral service may take place at the graveside, or in a mosque or in any open space.

Women attend Muslim funerals only if they are closely related to the deceased. Non-Muslims who wish to send flowers may do so.

Burial at sea

In rare instances there are requests for burial at sea. As at law this constitutes 'removal from the country', there are special formalities to fulfil. The first duty is to inform the coroner and to obtain his acknowledgment of receipt of notice of the intended removal. Arrangements can then usually be made through the funeral director and the nearest harbour master for chartering a vessel to take the coffin to sea. The vessel must proceed to a point outside the three-mile limit before the coffin can be committed to the deep, and the captain should be consulted about a suitable position, bearing in mind his knowledge of the currents and the tides. It is usual for a short religious service to be held on board at the time of the committal.

The return home

While the funeral is taking place, those left at home should discreetly remove all visible signs of sickness and sorrow. If the blinds have been drawn—they seldom are nowadays—they should be raised. It is less painful to return home to a bright house than to one exuding gloom.

These occasions draw together old friends and distant members of the family, and although it is no longer customary to provide luncheon, some form of refreshment should be offered to those who have travelled some distance to the funeral, before they set out on the return journey. It is usual for close relatives to extend a quiet invitation to such friends and relations as the mourners leave the graveside or view the flowers in the crematorium cloister. Those accepting should not stay too long, since solitude and quiet may often offer the only solace to the bereaved who are trying to maintain their composure in the face of grievous personal loss, but at the same time it is natural that at such a reunion a reasonably cheerful if subdued atmosphere should prevail.

144

Memorial services

When as often happens, a person is buried at some distance from their home, it is usual for the family to attend the funeral while a memorial service is held in the home parish church to coincide with the time of burial. Attendance at this service is regarded as equivalent to attending the funeral.

It is more usual, however, for a memorial service to take place a week or more after the funeral, particularly when this has been a strictly private affair for the immediate family only. A formal press announcement should appear at the time of, or a few days after, the death. No other cards or notices need be sent.

> SMITH—A memorial service for John J. Smith will be held at All Souls Church, Langham Place, London W.1., on Tuesday March 5, at 12 noon.

Letters of condolence

Letters of condolence should be sent as soon as a death is announced. They should be short and sincere, containing nothing which does not bear on memories of the person who has died and sorrow for those who are grieving. Such letters are extremely personal, and only the most general guide can be offered.

My dear Jane,

My husband and I are deeply grieved to hear of your sad loss and hasten to offer our condolences. John was such a beloved person and had so many fine qualities. The community has lost a great deal by his passing. While our sadness and sense of loss can do little to assuage your grief at this time, please believe that our loving thoughts are with you and don't hesitate to call on us if there is any practical help we can give. We pray you will be given strength in this great ordeal.

Your loving friend ——

Dear Miss Black,

I was deeply grieved to hear of your sister's death. She was so gay and bright and she will be sadly missed by all who knew and loved her. Please accept my deepest sympathy and be assured that my thoughts are with you at this sad time.

Yours sincerely ——

A personal letter of thanks should be sent to the writer of each letter of condolence, although if the number is considerable and the bereaved unable to undertake this at once, a notice can be put in the personal column of the local or national papers.

> Mrs A. Jones wishes to express her thanks for the many letters and lovely flowers sent to her on her recent bereavement. She will reply personally as soon as possible.

145

The replies should be sent within a month of the funeral. Something like this is a possible draft:

Dear Mrs Smith,

Your kind letter brought me great comfort in my desolation. It is hard to realise that my husband has gone and I am too bewildered as yet to grasp fully all that means, but I am strengthened for the future by the knowledge that your thoughts and prayers are with me. In his quiet way John did so much for others and I am proud to hear that his work did not pass unnoticed and that my loss is only part of a greater loss felt by those who knew him.

With many thanks for your understanding and kindness.

Yours sincerely ——

A note of thanks should also be written to anyone who sent flowers.

And afterwards

It is usual for the funeral director to pay all the fees and charges during the funeral arrangements, and for the family to settle his account afterwards. This will normally cover the removal of the body to a chapel of rest, assuming that this is within ten miles, the preparation of the body and the use of the private chapel, the coffin, the hire of the hearse and of a car for the chief mourners, the placing of press notices, the obtaining of the certificates, and the making of all church, cemetery and cremation arrangements, the bearers and attendance throughout the ceremonies (naturally the more elaborate the funeral, the higher the cost); at present, this would cost about £150. In addition there are statutory fees to be paid to the vicar, the clerk, the sexton and the parish church council, and the organist; the Death Grant (page 139) should cover all these.

The funeral director can advise the next-of-kin or the executor on the disposal of the ashes. This is usually decided a few days after cremation. The ashes may be buried or scattered; this is frequently done at the Garden of Rest attached to the crematorium, the immediate family attending.

If the family wishes to see a report of the funeral in the local paper, a short report can be written up, on the usual lines, and sent to the news editor, with a covering letter so that he can confirm the details if necessary.

Memorial notices can be inserted in the personal columns of the local and national papers. Gravestones and other memorials may be set up, subject to the approval of the cemetery or churchyard authorities, a year or so after burial; the design and wording should be checked in advance with the authorities. Several methods of memorial inscription are available at crematoria, including Books of Remembrance, wall tablets, inscribed flagstones and memorial vases. Many people like to give a shrub or a flowering tree.

To Help the Living

The Will

The making of a Will has already been discussed on page 43. A properly made Will eases and simplifies the task which falls upon the bereaved family, and can in itself be a comfort to them, showing that the deceased wanted to leave everything in order, and to save them any undue difficulty.

The next-of-kin will need to establish at once whether a Will exists. It is usual for anyone making a Will to ask those nominated as executors whether they are willing to stand, and to tell them where the Will is kept. If this has not been done, the next-of-kin should contact the solicitor and the bank to ask whether they have a Will in keeping.

Assuming that the deceased person has left a Will, this will be opened and read, and the solicitor will normally inform the beneficiaries. The Will has to be 'proved' before the District Probate Registry of the High Court of Justice for the district concerned. If the Will is thus proved to be the lawful act of the deceased person, **the Court grants probate** to the executors named in the Will and they are then able to administer the estate. It will take several months to get probate on a straightforward Will; if a business or a trust fund or anything else is involved, it will usually take a good deal longer.

If anyone dies without having made a Will, he or she is said to have died 'intestate'. Application has then to be made to the Court, usually by the next-of-kin, for permission to administer the estate. The Court, when satisfied as to the claims of the applicant, issues **Letters of Administration,** appointing the applicant as administrator of the estate. This too takes time.

Other essentials

While awaiting probate or letters of administration, the next-of-kin or executor should inform the bank (do this immediately to stop payment of cheques and banker's orders), and the post office if the deceased had a post office savings account. Notify the deceased's employers, any insurance companies with which he held policies, any Building Society, and so on. Tell the tax inspector, and go to claim the Death Grant (page 139). Send back any pension or allowance books, with a covering letter claiming anything that is due. Send back the passport and driving licence. But do not sell or dispose of any property until probate or letters of administration are granted.

Benefits, pensions, allowances

In addition to the leaflet describing the Death Grant (NI 49), there are a number of other useful leaflets which are obtainable from every local office of the Department of Health and Social Security: Widow's Benefits (NI 13), Industrial Death Benefits for Widows and Other Dependants (NI 10), Retirement Pensions for Widows (NI 15A), Guardian's Allowance (NI 14), Child's Special Allowance (NI 93), Supplementary Pensions and Allowances (SB 1).

Donating one's body for anatomical examination or medical research
Anyone who wishes to donate his or her body for **anatomical examination** can leave instructions that after death it shall be sent to a school of anatomy for this purpose. The instructions may be made orally to executors, next-of-kin and family but it is better if the wishes are made known to them in writing. (This written statement should also stipulate whether ultimate cremation or burial is preferred.) It should be noted, however, that executors or next-of-kin are not bound to carry out the instructions for such bequests are not legally enforceable. To spare the next-of-kin distress and anxiety, these wishes should be made known well before death, to all who may be concerned, and clearly set down in writing—not in a Will, which may not be opened until after the funeral.

When the donor dies the usual formalities already described on pages 134–38 must be observed, and the executors or next-of-kin should telephone the Inspector of Anatomy or the Department of Anatomy of the nearest Medical School (any doctor can provide this information) to inform them of the bequest. The bequest *may* be refused, but if it is accepted the necessary forms will be supplied for completion and despatch and arrangements will be made for the removal of the body to the Medical School.

The death must, of course, be registered in the usual way before the body is removed. The undertaker who removes the body will take away with him the registrar's disposal certificate (and, where there is one, a special medical certificate which is supplied when the arrangements for donating the body are made with the Medical School direct).

The Medical School may retain the body for a period not exceeding two years after which they will normally make arrangements for burial or cremation in accordance with the custom of the religious denomination to which the deceased belonged. The expense of a simple funeral will be borne by the Medical School; if a more elaborate funeral is desired, the relatives may usually arrange for this but must meet the cost themselves.

Further information may be obtained by writing to HM Inspector of Anatomy at the Department of Health and Social Security in London, or to the Scottish Home and Health Department; addresses are given on page 157.

Alternatively a body may be bequeathed for **medical research** including **transplantation** under the Human Tissue Act 1961. Anyone wishing to

148

bequeath his or her body for this purpose should make a written statement of the request, copies of which should be given to the family or anyone else with whom he or she lives, and to the executor if he or she has made a Will. If ever the donor has to go into hospital as an in-patient he or she should tell the hospital staff that they have made this statement. Upon death, the family should ask the advice of the doctor in attendance at the time as in some circumstances it may not be possible to take advantage of the offer.

Donating kidneys

In 1974 Mrs Elizabeth Ward initiated a campaign to publicise the Kidney Donor Scheme introduced in 1972 by the Health departments of England, Scotland and Wales. The gift of healthy kidneys which may, by a transplant operation, bring new life to those who suffer from kidney disease is a notable bequest from the dead to the living; and anyone wishing to take part in this scheme should tell their next-of-kin and executors of their wish, and carry a Kidney Transplant Donor Card at all times, in case of accident. These cards are obtainable from one's family doctor, in hospital waiting rooms and universities. Kidneys must be taken within an hour of death if the transplant is to prove successful; to make one's wishes plain in advance, and to carry formal notification in one's wallet, can save vital time and spare the next-of-kin distress and anxiety.

Donating corneas

The grafting of corneas for the relief of blindness is covered by the Human Tissue Act of 1961. A leaflet entitled *Restore Sight* is obtainable from the Department of Health and Social Security in London or the Scottish Home and Health Department in Edinburgh, and this explains how eye surgeons are often able to restore sight to a blind person by replacing parts of his or her eyes with tissue from the eyes of someone who has just died. The leaflet incorporates four simple bequest forms: one to be given to the donor's family or to the person with whom he or she may be living, one to the executor of his or her Will (if he or she has made one), one to be given to the family doctor, and one to be sent to one of the organisations for the blind, a list of which is included. Friends or relatives should be told by the donor that he or she has made this bequest. Thus they will know, when the time comes, that the operation is carried out at the express wish of the deceased, in the hope that his or her corneas may give sight to those who live on—that it is, as it were, a pre-planned gesture of help. This can in itself be a source of comfort to the bereaved.

Honours and Decorations

The Victoria Cross (V.C.) and the George Cross (G.C.) take precedence over all other honours and decorations. They are immediately followed by membership of the first three Orders of knighthood; the Garter (K.G.), the Thistle (K.T.) and St Patrick (K.P.). Knights and Dames Grand Cross of the Order of the Bath (G.C.B.) are followed by the members of the Order of Merit (O.M.).

Then come the various classes of the later Orders, including the lower classes of the Order of the Bath: Knights Grand Commanders of the Order of the Star of India (G.C.S.I.), Knights and Dames Grand Cross of the Order of St Michael and St George (G.C.M.G.), Knights Grand Commanders of the Order of the Indian Empire (G.C.I.E.); the Imperial Order of the Crown of India, which is restricted to women (C.I.); Knights and Dames Grand Cross of the Royal Victorian Order (G.C.V.O.) and of the Order of the British Empire (G.B.E.); Companions of Honour (C.H.); Knights and Dames Commanders of the Orders of the Bath, the Star of India, St Michael and St George, and the Indian Empire, (K.C.B., D.C.B., and so on) in that order; Knights and Dames Commanders of the Royal Victorian Order and the Order of the British Empire (K.C.V.O. and D.C.V.O., K.B.E. and D.B.E.); Companions of the Bath and of the Orders of the Star of India, St Michael and St George, and the Indian Empire, (C.B., C.S.I., C.M.G., C.I.E.); and Commanders of the Royal Victorian Order and the Order of the British Empire (C.V.O., C.B.E.).

Then come, again in order, various decorations and medals, and membership of the lower classes of these Orders, and of other Orders: first the Distinguished Service Order (D.S.O.); membership of the fourth class of the Royal Victorian Order (M.V.O.): Officers of the Order of the British Empire (O.B.E.); the Imperial Service Order (I.S.O.); the fifth class of the Royal Victorian Order (M.V.O. again); and Members of the Order of the British Empire (M.B.E.). The Royal Red Cross first class (R.R.C.) ranks immediately before the Distinguished Service Cross (D.S.C.), the Military Cross (M.C.), the Distinguished Flying Cross (D.F.C.), and the Air Force Cross (A.F.C.), and the second class (R.R.C. again) immediately before the Albert Medal (A.M.) (now exchangeable for the George Cross), the Distinguished Conduct Medal (D.C.M.), the Conspicuous Gallantry Medal (G.G.M.), and the George Medal (G.M.).

Obtaining Birth, Adoption, Marriage and Death Certificates

England and Wales

The General Register Office is at St Catherine's House, 10 Kingsway, London WC2B 6JP. Its records go back to 1837, as do those held locally.

Birth, marriage and death certificates may be obtained either from the appropriate local register office or from the General Register Office. If supplied by the registrar by whom the birth, death or marriage was registered, a short birth certificate will cost 25p, and a standard birth, marriage or death certificate 50p. Once the register containing the required entry has been deposited with the superintendent registrar (this is done when the register is full), a short birth certificate will cost you 25p, a standard birth, marriage or death certificate 75p. Alternatively you can apply to the General Register Office. If you apply in person, you can either arrange to collect the certificate a few days later or alternatively have it posted to you, in which case the fees are again 25p for a short birth certificate and 75p for a standard birth, marriage or death certificate; if, however, you apply by post, there is an additional handling fee, which is at present 50p. Birth, marriage and death certificates are not normally obtainable from the General Register Office until about a year after the event was registered.

If the marriage was not registered by a registrar, a marriage certificate may be obtained from the church, chapel or place where the marriage was solemnised.

Applications for certificates from the Adopted Children Register should be made to the Registrar General, General Register Office, Segensworth Road, Titchfield, Fareham, Hampshire, PO15 5RU. The short certificate costs 25p, the standard one 75p.

Scotland

The General Register Office is at New Register House, Edinburgh EH1 3YT. Its statutory records go back to 1855 but it also has parochial registers, the earliest entry in which dates back to 1553.

Extracts of entries in the birth, marriage and death registers held by that office and by local registrars can be obtained for a fee of 50p. Abbreviated certificates of birth, which show no details of parentage, cost 20p. The public can also carry out searches of the indexes to the registers for additional fees which vary according to the amount of searching carried out or the time spent on searching. Extracts from adopted children registers or parochial registers held by the General Register Office may also be obtained on payment of the prescribed fee.

Northern Ireland

The General Register Office is at Oxford House, 49–55 Chichester Street, Belfast BT1 4HL.

The birth and death records go back to 1864. Birth and death certificates, and certificates from the Adopted Children Register, may be obtained from the General Register Office. Birth and death certificates for registrations made within the previous twelve months can also be obtained from the registrars.

Roman Catholic marriage records go back to 1864 and other marriage records to 1845. Copies from 1922 only are held in the General Register Office. Original registers from 1845 are in the custody of the registrars (there are twenty-six registrars, their offices being, in the main, in the principal towns) and of the clergy; the General Register Office will, however, generally obtain certificates on behalf of applicants. Marriage certificates of more recent date can be obtained either from the General Register Office or from local registrars.

Addresses and Fees at the Time of Publication

The Professions

The General Medical Council,
44, Hallam Street, London W1

The Law Society,
113 Chancery Lane, London
WC2A 1PL

The Royal Institute of
British Architects,
66, Portland Place, London
W1N 4AD

The Royal Institution of Chartered
Surveyors,
12 Great George Street, London
SW1P 3AD

Incorporated Society of Valuers and
Auctioneers,
3 Cadogan Gate, London SW1X 0AS

Clothes

Moss Bros.
Bedford Street, Covent Garden, London WC2E 8JB (01–240 4567) Branches at Aldershot, Birmingham, Bournemouth, Bradford, Brighton, Bristol, Camberley, Cambridge, Cardiff, Cheltenham, Chester, Croydon, Dorking, Edinburgh, Exeter, Glasgow, Hanley, Henlow, Hull, Ilford, Kingston upon Thames, Leeds, Leicester, Liverpool, London (Lime Street), Luton, Maidstone, Manchester, Newcastle upon Tyne, Norwich, Nottingham, Plymouth, Reading, Salisbury, Sheffield, Southampton, Southsea, Swansea, Watford, Wolverhampton, York, Paris.
Wedding gowns from about £9 to about £50, plus 49p postage and packing; fur stoles from £6.50, a mink jacket £15, a fur coat from £14 to £24, all plus packing and carriage; riding boots £4.75 a day, and £2.40 on successive days; wet suits for diving or sailing, £4.45 for a week-end, water skis £5.00, snorkel, £1.55, life jacket £2.10, sailing jacket and trousers, £4.85: all inclusive of V.A.T.

Cameo Corner,
26 Museum Street, London WC1
Jewellery for hire at terms based on 10% of the value of the article per day, minimum charge of £2.50, plus a deposit for the full value; hirer responsible for insurance.

Young's Dress Hire,
178–180 Wardour Street, London W1
Specialise in wedding and evening wear for hire

To Obtain A Passport
The regional Passport Offices are as follows:

The Passport Office,
Clive House, 70 Petty France,
London SW1H 9HD (01 222 8010)
 For those living in London, Middlesex

Foreign and Commonwealth Office Passport Agency, Marlborough House, 30 Victoria Street, Belfast BT1 3LY (Belfast 32371).
 For those living in Northern Ireland; but no postal applications or correspondence can be dealt with (see below)

Passport Office,
Empire House, 131 West Nile Street, Glasgow G1 2RY (041 332 0271)
 For those living in Scotland, and for postal applications from Northern Ireland

Passport Office,
India Buildings, Water Street, Liverpool L2 0QZ (051 227 3461)
 For those living in Anglesey, Caernarvonshire, Cheshire, Cumberland, Denbighshire, Derbyshire, Durham, Flintshire, Lancashire, Merionethshire, Northumberland, Staffs, Westmorland, Yorkshire

Passport Office,
Olympia House, Upper Dock Street, Newport (Mon.), NPT 1XA (Newport 52431)
 For those living in Berks, Breconshire, Cardiganshire, Carmarthenshire, Cornwall, Devon, Dorset, Glamorgan, Gloucestershire, Hampshire, Herefordshire, Monmouthshire, Montgomeryshire, Oxfordshire, Pembrokeshire, Radnorshire, Shropshire, Somerset, Surrey, Sussex, The Isle of Wight, Wilts, Worcs.

Passport Office,
Westwood, Peterborough, PE3 6TG P'boro 263636)
 For those living in Beds, Bucks, Cambs, Essex, Herts, Huntingdonshire, Leics, Lincs, Norfolk, Northants, Notts, Rutland, Suffolk, Warwickshire.

At present, the Belfast Office is open from Monday to Friday, from 9.30 in the morning until 4.30 in the evening, and the others from Monday to Friday, 9.00 in the morning until 4.30 in the evening. In addition there is a duty officer to deal with emergency cases only: from 4.30 to 6.00 on Mondays to Fridays, and from 10.00 to 12 noon on Saturdays, Sundays and public holidays, at the **London** office; and from 4.30 to 5.30 Mondays to Fridays and 10.00 to 12 noon on Saturdays at **Glasgow, Liverpool, Newport** and **Peterborough.**

The present fees are £1.50 for a British Visitor's passport, valid for a year only and not renewable, and £5 (30 pages) or £10 (94 pages) for a United Kingdom passport, valid for ten years.

The British Visitor's passport is valid only for short visits within the year of issue. The holder must not take up employment in the country he visits. Denmark, Finland, Greenland, Iceland, Norway and Sweden form a common travel area recognising the Visitor's passport, but visits to the area must not exceed three months in any nine-month period; Canada also recognises it, for visits not exceeding three months, but additionally requires that it must be valid for three months beyond the last date the traveller will be in Canada; Andorra, Austria, Belgium, France, the Federal Republic of Germany (but *not* the German Democratic Republic), Gibraltar, Greece, Italy, Liechtenstein, Luxembourg, Malta, Monaco, the Netherlands, Portugal, San Marino, Spain and Switzerland and Turkey, all recognise it for visits not exceeding three months. A holder may travel to or from any of these countries via the Republic of Ireland, but may not pass en route through any other countries (as might, for instance, be the case if you were hoping to travel overland to Greece) which do *not* recognise the Visitor's passport.

The Marriage

The Faculty Office,
1 The Sanctuary, Westminster,
London SW1

The Office of the Chief Rabbi,
Alder House, Mezzanine Floor,
Tavistock Square, London WC1
(01–387 1066)

South Place Ethical Society,
Conway Hall, 25 Red Lion Square,
London WC1R 4RL (01–242 8032)

The Islamic Cultural Centre,
Regent's Lodge, Park Road,
London NW8 (01–723 7611)

The Buddhist Society,
58 Eccleston Square, London
SW1 1PH

At present the C. of E. fee for the publication of banns is £1.05 per parish, and the certificate of banns (that is, confirmation that the banns have been read in the second parish) costs another 70p. The statutory fee for the ceremony without organ music is £4, with organ music £8; this does not include the organist's fee. The fees for other services—the choir, the bells, heating the church and so on—vary from parish to parish. The marriage certificate costs 50p, additional certificates ordered at the same time 10p each (these may be needed for tax, insurance and other purposes), and additional ones ordered at a later date, 40p each.

A common licence for a C. of E. wedding will cost £4.50, a special licence £25 (this can be varied by the Legal Officer at the Faculty Office, if there is good reason), and a superintendent registrar's certificate £1 for entering notice plus possible extra fees; the fees for the church ceremony are as quoted above.

The fee for marriage by superintendent registrar's certificate will be about £4 (this includes the marriage certificate and the fee for entering notice), and for marriage by certificate and licence issued by a superintendent registrar, about £8 (again including the marriage certificate).

In Scotland, proclamation of banns costs 35p. The fee for each publication of notice of marriage by the registrar is 25p, and each certificate of publication costs 10p. The Court fee for a Sheriff's Licence is £2.50, and the solicitor's fee is additional. The fee payable to an authorised registrar for conducting a civil marriage is £1, and there may in addition be an accommodation booking fee if the marriage room facilities are above average. In the case of a church wedding, it is usual for a fee to be charged covering such overheads as lighting and heating, and the couple will generally make a gift to the minister as well. The marriage certificate costs 50p; copies ordered at the same time cost 30p each.

At present the fees in Northern Ireland are as follows: Notice 25p; Licence, £1; Certificate, 10p. If the registrar attends to register a marriage in a church or other building registered for the solemnisation of marriages, he must be paid 50p (marriage by registrar's certificate) or £1 (marriage by registrar's licence), plus his travelling expenses. The couple must also pay postage on copy notices and meet the cost of publication of their notice of marriage in a newspaper, where necessary. Depending on the mode of marriage followed, fees may also be payable to Church authorities.

A certificate of marriage issued by the Islamic Cultural Centre for a Muslim wedding costs £5.50. This fee is independent of the usual civil marriage fees paid to the superintendent registrar.

A fee of £6.30 is payable in respect of marriage authorisation at the Office of the Chief Rabbi. This is in addition to the usual civil marriage fees.

H.M. Inspector of Anatomy, Department of Health and Social Security, 16–19 Gresse Street, London W1 1PB.

Royal National Institute for the Blind, 224 Great Portland Street, London W1N 6AA

Scottish Home and Health Department, Eagle Buildings, 19 Rose Street, Edinburgh, EH2 2PR;

and for cornea donation St Andrew's House, Edinburgh EH1 3DE

Some Useful Books

Whitaker's Almanack, an independent publication which is packed with contemporary information on public affairs, the government, industry and finance, social usage, the arts, present legislation, societies and institutions, and so on. A new, up-to-date edition is published each year.

Montague-Smith, Patrick (Ed.), *Debrett's Peerage, Baronetage, Knightage and Companionage,* Kelly's Directories: information about the peerage, privy councillors, baronets, knights, companions of Orders, etc.; it also contains the Table of Precedence and a list of the Royal Warrant Holders.

Townend, Peter, *Burke's Peerage,* Burke's Peerage Ltd; genealogical and heraldic histories

Titles and Forms of Address, A. & C. Black, London

Who's Who, with useful paragraphs of biographical information, including honours and decorations held and, frequently, addresses; all its allied publications (*Who's Who in Music, Who's Who in the Theatre,* etc.); and *Who Was Who,* containing the brief biographical entries of those who appeared in earlier issues and who have since died.

Speeches and Toasts for all Occasions, W. Foulsham & Co. Ltd., 1972

Taylor, H. M. and Mears, A. G., *The Right Way to Conduct Meetings, Conferences and Discussions,* Elliot's Right Way Books, 1959

In addition, there are a number of publications such as the Law List (*barristers and solicitors*), the Medical Register (*doctors*), Crockford's (*Anglican clergymen*), The Navy List, *etc., which list the members of particular professions and callings; your local reference library will advise you on these, and should also be able to help you to find an informative book on almost any subject.*

Index